Changing Countryside in Britain

Martin K Duddin

Assistant Head Teacher
Knox Academy, Haddington

Alister J Hendrie

Assistant Head Teacher
Portobello High School, Edinburgh.

Edward Arnold

First published 1985
Reprinted 1986
by Edward Arnold (Publishers) Ltd
41 Bedford Square
London WC1B 3DQ

Edward Arnold (Australia) Pty Ltd
80 Waverley Road, Caulfield East
Victoria 3145, Australia

British Library Cataloguing in Publication Data
Duddin, Martin K.
    Changing countryside in Britain.
    1. Great Britain—Description and travel—1971–
    I. Title   II. Hendrie, Alister
    914.1   DA632
    ISBN 0-7131-7325-4

Filmset in Compugraphic 10/11pt Times by
CK Typesetters Ltd, Sutton, Surrey
and printed in Great Britain by
The Bath Press, Avon

Acknowledgements
The Publishers wish to thank the following for the
permission to use copyright photographs and material

Crown copyright/Cambridge University Collection
    p.24;
John Topham Picture Library pp.4, 34;
Derek Widdicombe pp.11, 18;
Bus and Coach Council p.14;
Martin Duddin p.15;
Cambridge University Collection of Aerial
    Photographs pp.31, 36, 62, 69, 79;
British Geological Survey pp.35, 68;
Geoffrey N. Wright p.38;
Yorkshire Dales National Park p.39;
Hywel Hughes p.46;
Image Photographic Services p.56;
Northumbrian Water Authority pp.57, 59;
Northumbria Air Fotos p.61;
Department of Physical Planning, East Lothian
    District Council pp.86, 87.
Her Majesty's Stationery Office and other sources for
    a map which appeared in *Water Resources in
    England and Wales* p.54;
Mrs Monkhouse for diagrams from F.J. Monkhouse
    The English Lake District p.78;
Ordnance Survey and Dyfed County Council for a
    map p.67;
The Bus and Coach Council p.14;

The authors wish to thank the many individuals and
organisations who gave help and suggestions for the
contents of this book, particularly:
Dr Ian Baugh, Nature Conservancy Council, Edinburgh
Philippe Destombes, Kimberly-Clark Limited.
B.R. Conlon, Northumbrian Water Authority
Alistair Clunas, John Muir Country Park, E. Lothian
Ian Fullerton, East Lothian District Council
Tom Gant, Dartmoor National Park
Isobel Gibson & Nic Bullivant, Lochore Meadows
    Country Park.
Roger Prescott, Hampshire County Council
Ron Sands, Lake District National Park
P.H. Begbie, Milford Haven Conservancy Board.

Special thanks are due to Mrs Irene Hendrie for
collating the glossary and to the staff and pupils of the
Geography Departments of Knox Academy
Haddington and Portobello High School, Edinburgh.

N.B. Capitalised words in the text are defined in the
Glossary on pp. 94–96.

Contents

1

The changing landscape

Most people in Britain, if asked to describe a 'natural landscape' would use an image of the type of scene in Fig. 1.1. Certainly, the area in question does not seem to be dominated by people. There are no settlements or communications evident, yet the landscape is far from being in its 'natural' state. Even in remote areas such as this, the rural landscape of Britain is essentially man-made — in this case the result of many centuries of hill farming, by which the action of people and their domestic animals have changed almost the entire face of these islands.

In order to fully appreciate the use made of the countryside, it is first necessary to look at the geological diversity from which the landscape around us takes its shape. As Fig. 1.3 indicates, although the British Isles cover only a small area, the underlying rocks change considerably over short distances, resulting in a variety of landscape found in few other countries of similar size. This book deals with some of the landscape types which have evolved in Britain, and the way in which people have used the landscape as a natural resource in their activities.

WEATHERING
All processes- mechanical, chemical and biological by which rocks are loosened and disintegrated by exposure to the elements.

↓

MASS MOVEMENTS
Downward movement of weathered material on a slope under the influence of gravity and usually lubricated by rain water or snowmelt

↓

EROSION
The sculpting of the earth's surface and scenery by water, wind or ice movement.

↓

TRANSPORTATION
Removal and movement of rock debris by the agents of erosion

↓

DEPOSITION
The laying down of material transported by running water, wind, ice and the sea.

1.2 Processes of landscape change

Changing physical landscape

It is important to remember at the outset that landscape is dynamic. It is not static, but is undergoing constant change. Britain is not a country of extremes, there are no active glaciers or volcanoes, no deserts to cause dramatic landscape changes. Nevertheless, the land surface is constantly altering, although mostly so slowly that we are seldom able to monitor major change within a human lifetime.

The main processes at work in shaping the scenery of Britain may be less spectacular, but

1.1 A 'natural landscape'

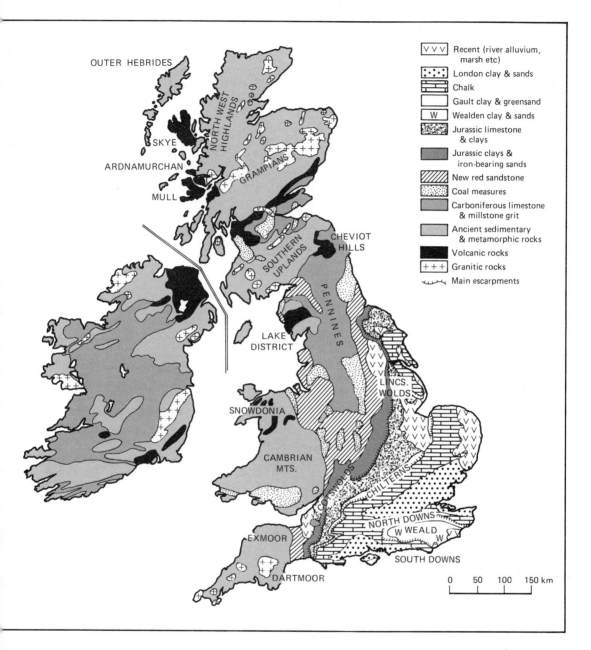

OUTER HEBRIDES

SKYE

ARDNAMURCHAN

MULL

NORTH WEST HIGHLANDS

GRAMPIANS

SOUTHERN UPLANDS

CHEVIOT HILLS

PENNINES

LAKE DISTRICT

SNOWDONIA

LINCS. WOLDS

CAMBRIAN MTS.

COTSWOLDS

CHILTERNS

NORTH DOWNS

W WEALD

EXMOOR

SOUTH DOWNS

DARTMOOR

V V V	Recent (river alluvium, marsh etc)
	London clay & sands
	Chalk
	Gault clay & greensand
W	Wealden clay & sands
	Jurassic limestone & clays
	Jurassic clays & iron-bearing sands
	New red sandstone
	Coal measures
	Carboniferous limestone & millstone grit
	Ancient sedimentary & metamorphic rocks
	Volcanic rocks
+++	Granitic rocks
	Main escarpments

0   50   100   150 km

.3 Geology of the British Isles

…hey are constantly active. The DENUDATION of …he land surface by a combination of natural …orces (Fig. 1.2) acting upon the variety of …eological structures which underlie the British …sles, gives our landscape its character and …ariation. Apart from geology, the climate of the …ountry, and its changes over time, has also played … vital role in shaping the landscape. Although the …st ice-age ended 10 000 years ago, weathering

and erosion by natural forces are still sculpting the earth's surface in Britain, although the extent to which they are successful is largely dependent upon the underlying rock types.

Most of the older and more resistant rocks are found in the north of Britain (Fig. 1.3), but in the far south-west, erosion and earth movement have exposed huge BOSSES of ancient granites. These igneous rocks give the area a varied and attractive scenery, appearing as rugged coastal headlands such as Land's End, bleak moorlands like Dartmoor (Chapter 2) and even islands such as the

Isles of Scilly. In Scotland the granites stand out as impressive mountain massifs such as the Cairngorms and the hills of Galloway.

Most of southern and eastern Britain is an accumulation of SEDIMENTARY materials, mud, shales, sand and shells which have created a patchwork of different landscapes (Chapter 3). These rocks were laid down when the land was covered with invading seas and include the limestones, notably the carboniferous limestones of the Pennines and the more recent deposits of jurassic limestone which extend from Dorset to Yorkshire in a broad band and have given rise to the Cotswolds.

Chalk also owes its origins to sedimentary deposits. When the land subsided and was covered by the Cretaceous seas, tiny marine organisms left their skeletons to create the expanses of chalk downlands when the seas receded.

Not all of the sedimentary rocks in Britain are of recent origin. As Fig. 1.3 shows, large areas of the north and west are underlain by ancient sedimentary and METAMORPHIC rocks. These were laid down between 500 and 1 000 million years ago and have undergone changes in form and mineral composition as a result of intense heat and pressure caused by earth movements. The gneiss and schist rocks which underlie the islands of the Outer Hebrides are of this type and are amongst the oldest rocks in Britain.

Eventually the land was uplifted from the sea by the mountain-building period which, by folding, also created the Alps. In the north-west of Scotland, active volcanoes were still pouring out lava in the Isle of Mull and the Ardnamurchan peninsula, but by this time the geological basis of much of our scenery was complete. It is the interaction between these rock patterns and agents of weathering and erosion which have created our modern landscape. Although water is the most active agent of erosion at work in the British landscape today, creating impressive river and coastal features (Chapters 5 and 6), the legacy of the ice-age is evident almost everywhere. Glaciers followed the patterns of the valleys which had been laid down by rivers millions of years before the Ice Age, but changed and modified them by use of massive erosive powers. Initially, the ice accumulated in the uplands of Scotland and Wales and eventually ice-sheets spread out to cover the entire country north of the Thames Estuary and Bristol Channel. As the climate became milder towards the end of the Ice Age, the ice receded, and huge glaciers moved down from the mountainous areas of the country such as the

Lake District and Snowdonia (Chapters 7 and 4 As they moved down the existing river valley they widened and deepened them, often creatin hugh troughs which later came to be occupied b lakes. In the lowlands, erosion was less markec but eventually huge spreads of sands and grave were deposited across the east of the country b the meltwaters beneath and flowing behin retreating glaciers.

Nothing so dramatic takes place today, but th physical landscape around us is far from static Weathering and erosion are still active, an constant change is still taking place, only mor slowly.

1. Outline and describe the main physical processe at work today in changing the British landscape

2. a) Using an atlas, together with Fig. 1.3 make a list c the following physical features and against eac write down the underlying geology of th appropriate area:
Isle of Lewis, Isle of Mull, Pennines, Yorkshir Wolds, The Fens, London Basin, The Weald South Downs.
   b) What general conclusion can be made about th different age of rocks in Britain between the nort and south of the country? How is this reflected i relief?
   c) Identify and explain any areas which ar exceptions to this statement.

3. Compare and contrast the effects of glaciation o upland and lowland Britain.

Changing land-uses

Earlier in this chapter we saw that even in th remotest parts of Britain, it is possible to identif the influence of people in changing the natura environment. Although the British landscape i clearly dominated by people, and the natural eco system has been progressively replaced, it does nevertheless, still contain elements which might b called WILDSCAPE. The land-use model Fig. 1. identifies three such 'scapes' ranging fror townscape - the continuously built up urban area through farmscape, where agriculture is th predominant land-use, to the wildscape, areas o heath, moor and forest which are dominated mor by nature than by people. The three 'scapes' ar separated by two 'fringe' zones which are ofte areas of land-use conflict. The marginal fringe between the wildscape and the farmscape, and th rural-urban fringe between the farmscape and th townscape. Developments in the townscape are are not within the scope of this book, but bot

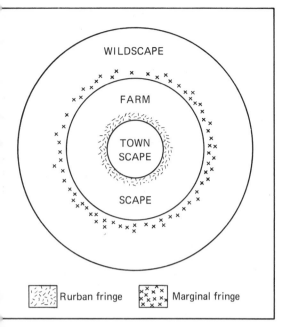

.4 Land-use in Britain

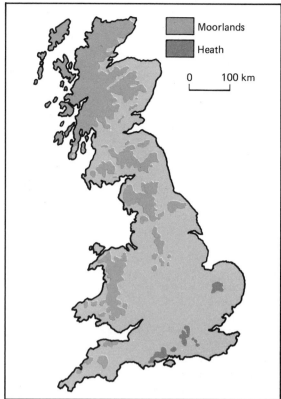

1.5 Distribution of heath and moorland in Britain

armscape and wildscape are undergoing onsiderable changes as the pressures upon them ncrease.

The changing wildscape

Moorland and heath together account for about ne-third of Britain's land area (Fig. 1.5) and in hese areas vegetation is dominated by heather, edges and grasses. The moorlands occupy those reas in which poor, thin soils and the wet climate ombine with altitude to generally limit any ultivation. As shown in Fig. 1.5 they are located articularly in the uplands of west and north-west Britain, extending from Bodmin and Dartmoor in he south-west, through Wales and northern England to the Scottish Highlands. The eathlands occur mainly in the lowland areas of outhern and eastern Britain, and are associated vith the sands and gravels of areas such as the Norfolk brecklands and New Forest.

Although these areas seem a natural part of the British landscape, in fact very little of this noorland or heath is original vegetation, and so he term wildscape, may be rather misleading. Old ocuments and early maps provide us with proof hat these areas were once occupied by extensive voodlands. Where these were cleared in rehistoric times, scientific analysis of pollen rains which have been preserved in peat deposits,

also reveal the former extent of woodlands now occupied by heath and moor.

As shown in Fig. 1.6, the decline of these ancient woodlands was the result of both natural and human induced changes, and the pace at which deforestation took place varied between the north and south of the country. In the south, population increase and the clearance of woodland for LANDAM farming, an early kind of shifting cultivation, took place as early as neolithic times. In contrast, clearance of parts of the huge Caledonian Forest in Scotland only took place during the eighteenth and nineteenth centuries as sheep farming expanded and demand for charcoal from the expanding iron industry grew. As the forests were cleared, the soil structure underwent considerable change and heath and moorland vegetation evolved as a result.

The continued existence of areas of heath and moorland in Britain up to the present day, is almost entirely due to continuous use and management by people. In those areas used for grazing sheep and cattle where vegetation may be burnt annually in order to replace it with new

7

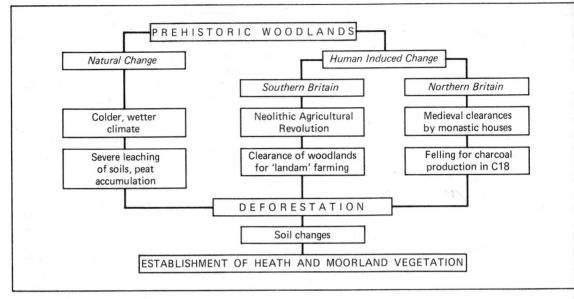

1.6 Evolution of heath and moorland vegetation in Britain

growth, this management is fairly obvious. Another traditional use of these areas was as Royal Forests — hunting grounds for the aristocracy. One such area is Exmoor which is the second smallest National Park in England and Wales and one of the few extensive areas of wildscape left in southern England. Its landscape has changed very little over the centuries as it was protected by the Crown as a Royal Forest. This status excluded most agricultural activities except for summer grazing, until enclosure in the early nineteenth century left 80% of the forest in private ownership. Initial attempts to introduce an arable rotation were unsuccessful but large tracts of moorland were transformed into good pasture. Reduction of moorland has continued with grants available from the Ministry of Agriculture and the European Community. The extent of moorland change was indicated by a report published in 1977 which recorded that 12 000 acres (4856 ha) of moorland were lost, of which 2 500 acres (1011 ha) went to woodland and the remaining 9 500 acres (3844 ha) were improved for agriculture.

Pressures on the wildscape such as this have resulted in the loss of its open character and while the re-establishment of forest might be regarded as a return to the natural vegetation, the huge coniferous plantations established in the north and west of Britain by the Forestry Commission and private landowners are frequently criticised for their artificiality. Agriculture and forestry are only two of the pressures being placed on wildscape areas. Others come from the popularity for recreational pursuits such as hillwalking, skiing and climbing. Chapter 4 looks in detail at these pressures on the Snowdonia area of north Wales.

In an attempt to restrict development, many areas of wildscape have been protected by designation as National Parks, National Nature Reserves or Sites of Special Scientific Interest (Chapter 7). The most recent attempt to give further protection was the 1982 Wildlife and Countryside Act which allows for compensation to be paid to private landowners who agree not to improve their land, but leave it as wildscape. Even so, the high cost involved in preserving such areas may mean that schemes such as that announced in 1983 to develop the Halvergate Marshes (Britain's finest remaining expanse of wild marshland in the heart of the Norfolk Broads) may go ahead unless society decides that it is prepared to pay for preserving such areas for future generations.

4. Describe and account for the distribution of wildscape in Britain.

5. Using Fig. 1.6 describe the changes which resulted in the evolution of heath and moorland from the original woodlands.

6. Outline the main pressures on the British wildscape today, referring to specific examples in your answer. What attempts are being made to protect such areas and how successful are these?

The changing farmscape

Although archaeologists suggest that people were living in the British Isles as long as about 200 000 years ago, their lives as primitive hunters and fishermen probably made little impact on the natural landscape until about 5000 years ago when the earliest forms of farming began to appear. In order to farm, the natural woodland had to be cleared and it was not until the New Stone Age that primitive technology allowed these clearances to take place — the first real success people had in changing their natural environment.

Ordnance Survey maps of most parts of Britain carry evidence of ancient settlements and field systems, but it was with the Roman Conquest that the most far reaching changes came. Extensive areas of the Fenlands of eastern England were reclaimed from marshland for agriculture and commercial farming was developed using the new road network to supply food to the defensive outposts in the north. In the south, London was already affecting land-use patterns by drawing on new farms in Sussex for its food supply. Although some farmland was abandoned during the Saxon period, by the time of the Norman Invasion of 1066, much of the settlement pattern of rural England had already been established.

As a result of rising population, agriculture became more intensive, so that by the twelfth and thirteenth centuries, open-field farming had developed: a few huge fields laid out in long, narrow strips and centred around a village. With less population pressure, the pace of change in Scotland, Wales and Ireland was rather slower, but most areas near to settlements developed farming systems and the surrounding landscapes were modified by farming patterns.

During the fifteenth century many landlords changed over to sheep farming to take advantage of booming wool exports and the new cloth industry. In the landscape, the deserted village became a common feature as the open-fields were converted to pasture and settlements abandoned. Later, the enclosure movement of the eighteenth century swept away the medieval pattern of the remaining open fields, as they were replaced with hedged rectangular fields with the new feature in the landscape — the isolated farmhouse away from the old village pattern. In all, about 18 million hectares were enclosed between 1760 and 1815 as the cultivated area was expanded to cope with increased demand for food as Britain moved into the Industrial Revolution. Uplands in the north and west were reclaimed from wastelands,

and areas of heath and chalk downlands in the south were also brought under the plough. By the 1850s the use of machinery was widespread and this changing technology has continued to be the main theme of agricultural change in Britain.

For most British industries, the period since 1945 has been one of mixed fortunes - of periods of 'boom' and 'recession'. In contrast, the post war years have been a time of unparalleled growth and change in farming, sometimes called the 'Second Agricultural Revolution'. From being a labour-intensive occupation with over 1 250 000 farmworkers and with more horses than tractors in use on British farms in 1950, Britain has developed one of the world's most advanced, mechanised and capital intensive farming systems, shown on Fig. 1.7. At the same time, the structure of the country's farming units has seen substantial change. The traditional image of the farm held by most of us, owes more to the 1930s than to the reality of the 1980s. Modern farms are not only more mechanised, and capital intensive with a smaller workforce, but also much larger as the small farmer has been replaced by the modern 'agri-business'. These changes are most noticeable in lowland Britain and in many cases have been accompanied by the loss of the traditional farming landscape features, most notably, trees, hedges, woodlands, stone walls and traditional building styles.

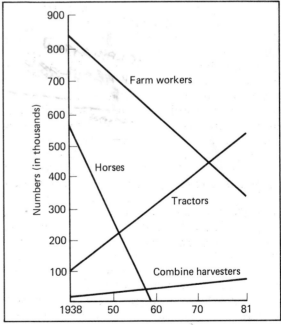

1.7 The effects of mechanisation on British farming

The crops grown and animals reared on our farms have also changed. Despite the loss of much prime agricultural land, especially in the rural-urban fringe, farmers have been able to produce more crops as fertilizers have contributed to higher yields, (Fig. 1.8), and low return crops such as oats have been replaced by wheat and barle (Fig. 1.9), and new crops such as oil-seed rape Alongside new crops are new breeds of cattle an sheep introduced from abroad and crossed wit our native breeds to produce a better quality an quantity of meat. Increased production has bee achieved by land improvement schemes involvin drainage, irrigation and reclamation, often wit assistance of grants from the government an European Community. Britain has now achieve 70% self-sufficiency in temperate foodstuffs. Th changes which have occurred in our landscape as result of the scale and nature of modern farmin are seen by many conservationists as threatenin the very character of the traditional British rura landscape.

(a) U.K. average crop yields (in tonnes per hectare)		
Crop	1938	1981
Wheat	2.2	6.2
Barley	2.0	4.6
Oats	1.9	4.3
Potatoes	14.5	32.8
(b) Livestock Numbers (millions)		
Cattle	8.6	13.1
Sheep	25.0	32.1
Pigs	4.5	7.8

1.8 Changing farming patterns

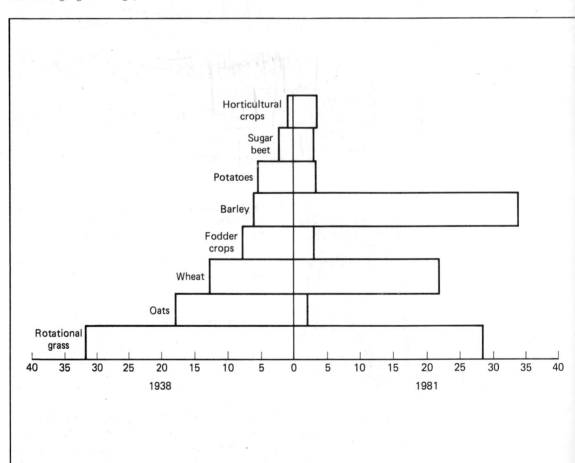

1.9 Major crops (as % of total cropland)

1.10 'An English village'

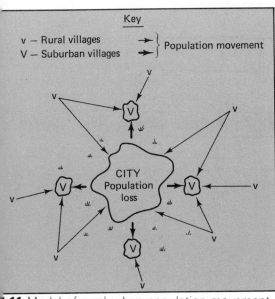

Key

v – Rural villages
V – Suburban villages

→→ } Population movement

CITY
Population
loss

.11 Model of rural-urban population movement

7. Draw a table summarizing the main changes which took place in the British farmscape between the Roman Invasion and the Second World War.

8. Explain why the pace of change has been much greater since 1945, and outline the trends shown by Fig. 1.7.

The changing village

It would be very difficult to imagine a scene more unchanging and typically English than the village scene in Fig. 1.10. Yet this nostalgic image is both outdated and inaccurate. Throughout Britain, villages were mostly created by people in the farmscape to fulfil an agricultural function which has become increasingly less relevant as the farm labour force has declined. The pace of change in villages has increased since 1945 as, depending on their locations, some have seen growth, whilst many others, perhaps the majority, have declined.

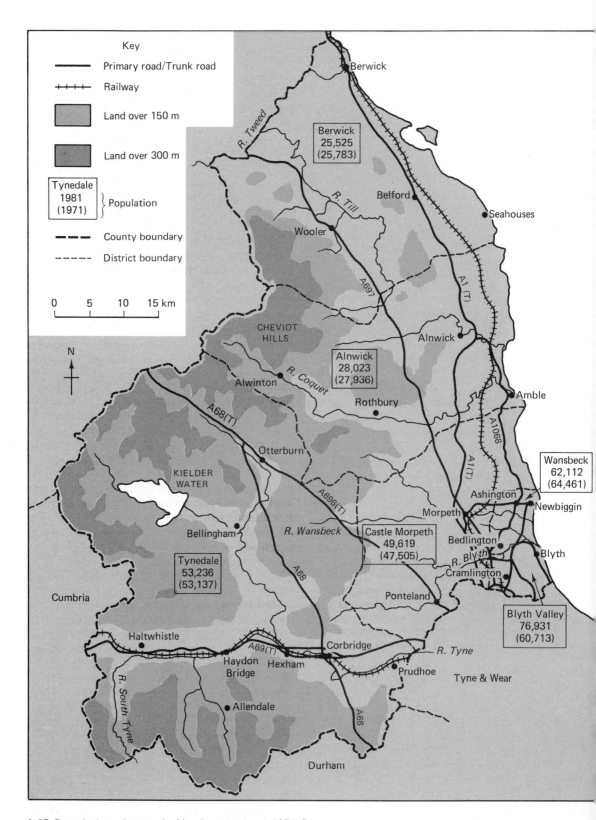

Key

Primary road/Trunk road
Railway
Land over 150 m
Land over 300 m

Tynedale
1981
(1971) } Population

County boundary
District boundary

0 5 10 15 km

N

Berwick

R. Tweed

Berwick
25,525
(25,783)

Belford

Seahouses

R. Till

Wooler

A697

A1 (T)

CHEVIOT
HILLS

R. Coquet

Alnwick
28,023
(27,936)

Alnwick

Alwinton

Rothbury

Amble

A68(T)

A1068

Otterburn

A1(T)

KIELDER
WATER

A696(T)

Wansbeck
62,112
(64,461)

Ashington

Newbiggin

Morpeth

Bellingham

R. Wansbeck

Castle Morpeth
49,619
(47,505)

Bedlington

Blyth

Tynedale
53,236
(53,137)

A68

R. Blyth

Cramlington

Cumbria

Ponteland

Blyth Valley
76,931
(60,713)

Haltwhistle

A69(T)

Corbridge

R. Tyne

Haydon
Bridge

Hexham

Prudhoe

Tyne & Wear

R. South Tyne

A68

Allendale

Durham

1.12 Population change in Northumberland 1971-81

As Fig. 1.11 shows, some villages near to major urban centres have grown rapidly as they have found a new role in accommodating the growing commuter population. Many people prefer to live in pleasant rural surroundings, yet retain access to the employment, shopping and entertainment facilities offered by the city. In contrast, those villages in more remote areas have continued to lose population as young people in particular are attracted away to the cities for greater employment opportunities. Using this approach, it is possible to identify two types of changing village in our countryside today: the truly rural village, and the suburban village.

The rural village: Northumberland

In the 1981 Census, Northumberland was the most sparsely populated county in England with an average population density of 0.6 persons per hectare. This average disguises the real distribution which varies from the highly urbanised areas of Blyth Valley and Wansbeck Districts to the bleak moorlands of the north Pennines and Cheviot Hills as shown in Fig. 1.12. The map also shows population change between the 1971 and 1981 Census and reveals that much greater increases took place in the areas next to the Tyneside conurbation in the south-east, than in the rural districts in the north and west of the country. In fact, in 1983 a survey undertaken for the Countryside Commission showed that the uplands of Northumberland were losing population more quickly that any other comparable area of Britain. These areas, over 250 metres above sea level, experienced a population loss of 30% between 1951 and 1981.

Employment Rural decline begins with falling job opportunities in the countryside and in the Northumberland uplands, heavily dependent on primary occupations such as farming and forestry, over 500 jobs have been lost in these employment categories between 1975 and 1981. Smaller rural communities have been particularly affected by these losses. This trend is not adequately revealed by Fig. 1.12. Although the three districts of Berwick, Alnwick and Tynedale show very little population change, in fact there have been considerable changes resulting in an internal redistribution of the county's rural population. Small communities such as Alwinton, high in the Cheviots, which has seen its population fall from 220 in 1931 to less than 100 today, continue to lose population, while the market towns, such as Hexham and Berwick, able to offer small-scale

industries, have actually seen population growth. In Alwinton, agriculture provided the mainstay of employment, but jobs in this sector have declined from 71 in 1925 to 21 in 1976. Population decline has been accelerated by the pull of jobs in the towns with higher rates of pay, more social hours of work and greater amenities.

Employment in forestry has also begun to contract in north Northumberland as the industry follows the same capital-intensive trends as farming. Investment by the Forestry Commission and private contractors in labour-saving machinery has cancelled out the job advantages formerly brought to rural areas.

The situation in Northumberland has been made worse by government industrial policy. Most of the rural areas of the county no longer qualify for industrial development grants and this means that any new companies attracted into the area are likely to locate in the urban areas of south-east Northumberland. This hinders still further the effort to deal with the social and economic problems of the rural areas. More recently, there are signs that these problems are being officially recognised. Although tourism has brought jobs to some rural areas, these may be seasonal and few in number. In an attempt to attract industry, organisations such as the Development Commission and CoSIRA — the Council for Small Industries in Rural Areas, have been set up. One of the most far reaching rural development projects has been the Integrated Development Programme for the Outer Hebrides of Scotland, jointly financed by the government and the European Community. A total of £20 million will be spent between 1982–87 to:

— Improve land and livestock
— Create marketing and processing projects
— Improve infrastructure
— Improve facilities for the fishing industry

A very important feature of this scheme is that it builds on, and develops, the existing traditional industries of the area, rather than attempting to impose new, and perhaps inappropriate industries on the area.

Transport The 1981 Census indicated that over 50% of households in Northumberland do not have access to a car. In the urban areas on the edge of the Tyneside conurbation, with frequent bus services and access to the new Tyneside Metro service, this may not be a major problem, but in the remoter parts of the county there are now often too few residents to justify the cost of providing even basic bus services. With branch railway lines now just a memory, it is estimated

An everyday story of countryfolk.

1. Since the village bus service was axed, young Jack Norris has had to leave his home and friends in order to live nearer his job, 12 miles away. It's a shame the way the old place keeps losing so many of its young people.

2. The village bus service was so handy for Mrs. Payne. It meant that whatever she couldn't buy in the village, she could always get in the next town. Now there's no bus, she's got a problem. Not to mention a 3 mile walk. Because in common with 70% of British women, Mrs. Payne does not have a driving licence.

3. Like a lot of young people today, Alan Murphy can't get a job. And now, he doesn't even have the means to go after one, because he's got no bus service either. No bus. No job. No hope. Alan is finding village life more and more frustrating.

4. Mrs. Sarah Smith (68 last birthday) used to rely on the village bus to take her to the doctor's surgery. Now the bus service has gone, she either has to beg a lift or take a six mile hike. It seems that when you live in the country, you have to be fit to be ill.

5. Ted Armitage hasn't been on a bus in years. Hasn't needed to with the car. But he's far from happy about the effect the lack of a bus service is having on the village. Ted runs the local shop — and it's not good for business the way people keep packing and leaving. And then there's his old ma. She used to rely on the bus a lot. Now she's going to be relying an awful lot more on Ted and his car.

6. It's not little Jane Harding's fault that her new secondary school is 2½ miles away from the village. But it's her problem. Because Jane's parents can't afford to run a car and the bus that took her to school has run its last journey. Now she has to bike it. And that's not much fun in the winter.

7. Tracey Cole is 17 and she's had it with village life. There was never much to do there anyway, but now the bus service has gone, she and her mates feel marooned. Never mind what her parents say, she's off to the bright lights and the big city just as soon as her bags are packed.

These stories represent the kind of problems faced by today's countryfolk. What's to be done to help them? This was one of the topics discussed by a wide range of community interests at a recent Convention in London.

1.13 The decline of transport in rural areas (Bus and Coach Council advertisement, 1984)

that between 25% and 33% of country people suffer an isolation unprecedented since the age of the stage coach. Old people may virtually become prisoners in their own village and simple journeys to shops, doctors or chemists become almost impossible (Fig. 1.13). Some small towns, such as Rothbury in Northumberland act as centres for postbus routes which combine mail collection and delivery with a basic bus service, but these are not available in all areas, and even these services have been withdrawn from some routes.

Services The decline in rural population has been matched by a steady reduction in the range of services provided for rural inhabitants. The village shop-cum-post-office has been affected by external factors. Those villagers with cars point to the high prices charged by the local shop and bulk-buy instead at distant supermarkets, using home-freezers to store food. The shop custom is reduced and it may even be forced to close — causing severe hardship for those without cars and unable to shop elsewhere. Although there are no national statistics available, county surveys recently indicated that over 40% of rural shops have closed since 1945, and that number increases each week. In some remote rural areas, local groups have formed community shops run by volunteers. In the Outer Hebrides, this idea has gone further with community co-operatives being formed with help from the Highlands and Islands Development Board. As well as providing general retailing, (Fig. 1.14), the activities of many of these groups include hire of farm machinery, knitwear production and building construction. They are proving to be valuable multi-functional businesses run for local benefit and controlled by the community within which they operate.

Cuts in local authority expenditure have hit even basic rural services such as mobile libraries and even rural telephone boxes are under threat in some areas. Almost every week, newspapers carry reports of the closure of village schools due to reduced pupil numbers — 76 schools were closed in rural areas of Britain in 1982 alone.

Housing Most people's image of country housing is limited to rambling, thatched cottages, but as many local authorities, including Northumberland move towards a 'key-settlement' policy, council house building in small villages is cut back or eliminated completely. Rather, the majority of new housing and employment opportunities are concentrated in the market

1.14 Barra Community Cooperative, Outer Hebrides

towns and urban areas, "where services can be maintained more effectively". This policy has clear implications for the scattered rural population as the smaller settlements continue to decline, and the price of private housing in them leaps out of the reach of local people because of the demand for second homes and holiday cottages by the urban population.

9. Identify the 'PUSH' and 'PULL' factors which are responsible for rural depopulation in areas such as north Northumberland.

10. Using Fig. 1.13, identify those sections of the rural population most likely to be affected by inadequate transport services.

11. Referring to specific examples describe what attempts are being made to encourage development in rural areas.

The suburban village

The 1981 Census revealed a general trend of population growth in many rural areas throughout Britain. This apparently contradicts what has been said earlier in this chapter, but in fact, the increase suggested by the census disguises the real trend in that over 30% of rural districts have continued to lose population and these losses have been almost entirely confined to the more remote areas. In contrast, those rural settlements which are within easy reach of main towns and cities have grown — often very rapidly.

In the post-war period as many of Britain's cities faced housing problems and growth in employment, they looked to neighbouring rural areas for residential land. As a result, many rural settlements have experienced pressures for development to accommodate a commuter population, and, with improved communications and increased car ownership, this 'dormitory' function of many villages has increased. An additional attraction for residents is that rates are often cheaper outside the city boundaries. As a result, the commuters can have all of the advantages of country life, whilst retaining access to all of the city's amenities.

This mixing of urban and rural land-uses in the 'fringe' areas between the townscape and the farmscape has not been without problems. Sporadic, unplanned development from the outer edge of cities into the rural areas tended to blur the distinction between town and country and brought with it large scale non-rural land-uses. The 'Green Belt' policy adopted by many cities has attempted to restrict developments which often took place on high quality farmland, but this has only been partially successful. Some cities have had no option but to use their surrounding farmscapes for housing overspill to relieve congestion in the city centres and allow urban redevelopment to take place. Some, like Carlisle in Cumbria, have identified several 'key villages' in the rural-urban fringe into which new development has been channelled. These are, generally, those settlements with adequate services, particularly water supply and sewage disposal facilities. The fringe settlements have certain characteristics in common:
— High proportion of post-war housing
— Low proportion of inhabitants working in the village
— High rate of car ownership
— Easy access to the urban area
— Relatively young population structure
— Poor provision of services within the village
— High loss rate of quality farmland.

The effects of Carlisle's policy are clearly evident from Fig. 1.15 which shows the five growth points in the city's fringe. Located to the north and east of the urban area, all have seen high population increases between 1971 and 1981. In contrast, the city itself, and the outlying rural parishes have continued to lose population. The trends revealed, of concentrating development and expansion in the larger rural settlements where services and access to employment are available, are being applied in most rural areas of Britain and have clear implications for the future of our more remote villages.

12. Outline what you understand by a 'Green Belt' policy and explain why they have been necessary in many parts of Britain.

13. Why have many villages in the 'rural-urban fringe' rapidly increased in population since 1945?

14. What are the main characteristics of these 'suburban villages'? How do these compare with the main features of 'rural villages?

15. Compare Fig. 1.15 with Fig. 1.11 and outline and explain any similarities and differences which you can observe.

16. What do you understand by a 'key settlement policy'? Explain why this is likely to contribute to the decline of the 'rural village'.

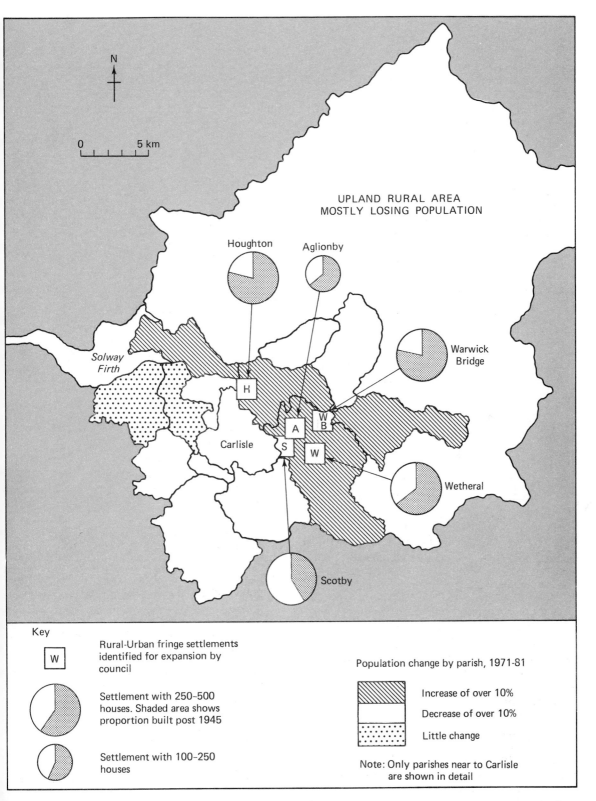

N

0 _____ 5 km

UPLAND RURAL AREA
MOSTLY LOSING POPULATION

Houghton   Aglionby

Solway
Firth

Warwick
Bridge

H

A
W B

Carlisle   S
          W

Wetheral

Scotby

Key

| W | Rural-Urban fringe settlements identified for expansion by council |

Settlement with 250–500 houses. Shaded area shows proportion built post 1945

Settlement with 100–250 houses

Population change by parish, 1971-81

Increase of over 10%

Decrease of over 10%

Little change

Note: Only parishes near to Carlisle
are shown in detail

1.15 Population change in North Cumbria 1971-81

2
Igneous landscapes

Igneous rocks have formed as a result of molten magma from deep inside the earth being forced up towards the surface through faults and fissures in the crust. Either on (EXTRUSIVE ROCKS) or just below (INTRUSIVE ROCKS) the earth's surface the magma cooled forming hard crystalline rocks such as basalt and granite respectively. These rocks are very resistant to erosion but after an extended period of time and exposure to the open air they do become susceptible to chemical weathering. The very slow rate at which these rocks weather has produced characteristic landscapes which occur in various areas throughout the British Isles (Fig. 2.1).

As igneous rocks are so resistant to erosion most igneous landscapes are well rounded uplands which are often covered with bleak moorland. In places the rounded profile of these uplands is

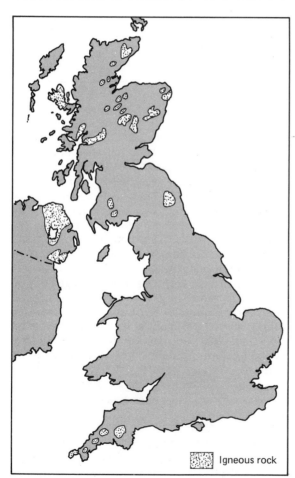

2.1 Main igneous rock areas of the U.K.

2.2

interrupted by 'tors' (Fig. 2.2), columns of widely jointed granite which have proved even tougher than the surrounding more narrowly jointed rock. Another distinctive feature often found below these tors is CLITTER, fragments of granite debris prized from the tors by freeze-thaw action.

In this chapter we are going to look at an example of an upland landscape formed largely on granite in south-west England. The back-bone around which Devon and Cornwall have formed consists of a series of inter-connected granite BOSSES (Fig. 2.3) which solidified originally as BATHOLITHS beneath the earth's surface and which have since been exposed to gradual denudation.

Case study of Dartmoor

Physical background The granite plateau of

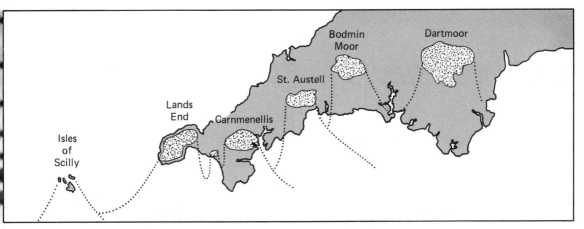

2.3 The inter-connected granite uplands of south-west England

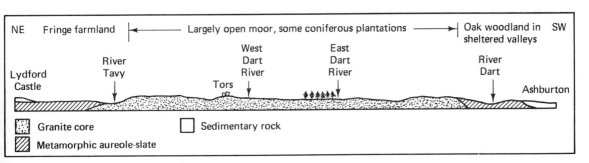

2.4 Cross-section through Dartmoor

Dartmoor (Fig. 2.4) rises at its highest point, High Wilhays, to over 600 metres (Fig. 2.5) and contains many of the features characteristic of igneous landscapes, including a large number of tors (Fig. 2.5). At the time when the batholith which now forms Dartmoor intruded below south-west England, the SEDIMENTARY ROCKS in close proximity were subjected to extreme heat and pressure or were 'metamorphosed'. Since that time, the surface layer of these METAMORPHIC ROCKS has been worn away, but those around the fringes remain, at least in part. Large scale land movements have tilted Dartmoor from north to south and this tilting has created a predominantly south-flowing river-pattern (Fig. 2.5). Dissection by these rivers means that the Dartmoor upland of today can be sub-divided into a larger and higher northern plateau, and a smaller and lower southern one. As Fig. 2.5 indicates, a lower-lying fringe area to the south and east can also be included within Dartmoor. These physical features could be typical of almost any igneous landscape or upland area in Britain. It is not, therefore, these general characteristics which make Dartmoor different, but rather the

way in which the flora and fauna and human activity have evolved which make it unique.

The core of the upland area is the moor itself which, lying close to the western seaboard of Britain at a relatively high altitude, tends to be bleak, wet and windswept and is covered with heather and grass. Another feature of this heartland, for which Dartmoor is infamous, are extensive blanket bogs, the largest of which is on the northern plateau. Around the fringes of the upland area deep gorges have been gouged out on the softer and less resistant rocks of the metamorphic aureole. These are the environments within which Dartmoor's indigenous 'hanging' oakwoods are still to be found, sometimes extending down from the edge of the upland itself, especially within the valleys of the Dart, Meavy, Teign and Walkham. Dartmoor is very fortunate to have retained such a large area of 'native' forest and it appears to be the only one of the ten National Parks in England and Wales in which 'the area under broadleaved trees substantially exceeds the area under alien conifers' (*Sandford Report*, 1974).

Plantations of conifers have, however, made

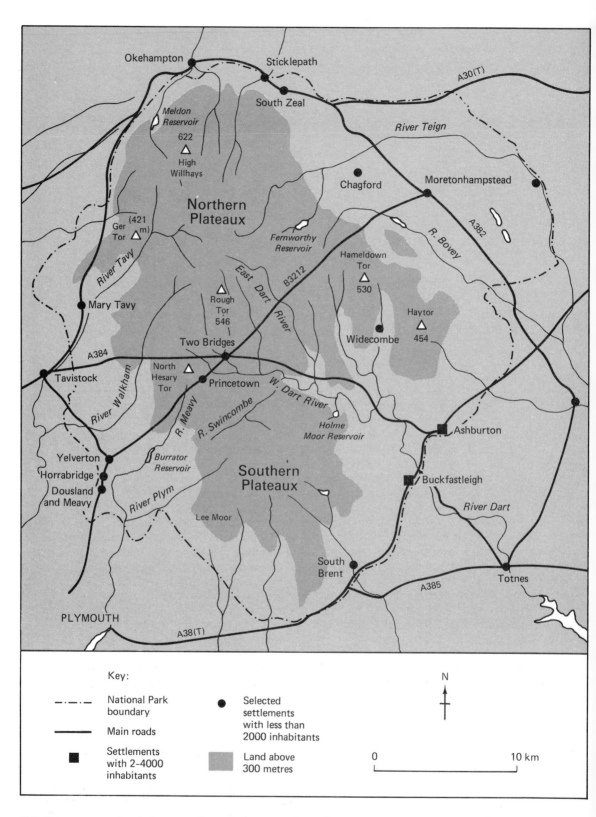

2.5 Dartmoor: upland, rivers, main setlements and roads

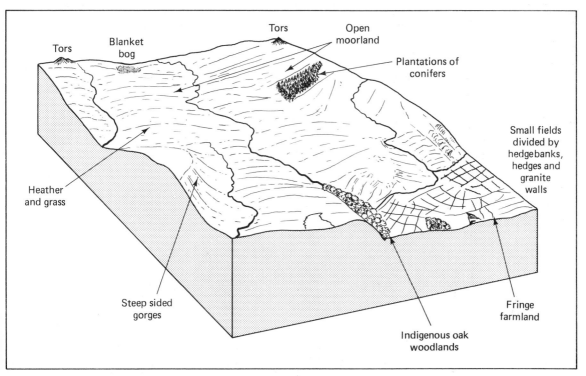

2.6 Annotated block diagram of Dartmoor landscape

some inroads into the native oakwoods and open moorland during this century. Initially the early plantings of conifers appeared to have little effect on the Dartmoor landscape but as these trees have grown and matured within geometrically shaped boundaries, dramatic changes have taken place. In particular, the plantings on the high moor gave rise to the most strident objections. These were so vociferous that there is little doubt that they contributed to the fact that only limited expansion of commercial forestry has taken place since, and those areas which have been newly planted have been carefully designed to blend in with the surrounding countryside. Perhaps the final piece in the unique jigsaw which fits together to create Dartmoor's landscape (Fig. 2.6), and perhaps that most obviously moulded by people, is the patchwork of small fields separated by hedgebanks and granite walls on the lower slopes.

Farming Farming practice through the centuries has been, and continues to be, the most important agent of landscape change. The physical nature of Dartmoor, including its poor quality, often peaty soils, has always placed severe restrictions on agriculture. Despite this, agriculture has always been the main industry on Dartmoor and remains the single most important employer, still acounting for about one job in five. As in most

other upland areas of Britain, the traditional type of agriculture has been hill farming and stock rearing which often involved the cultivation of crops in small fields near the farm for feeding to the stock during the winter months, and the grazing of COMMON LAND out on the moor in summer. 41% of Dartmoor is common land which is often privately owned and over which 'commoners' have had grazing rights since before the Norman Conquest. Although the traditional type of farming is now very much in decline, the right to graze stock on common land is still important to many farmers and has been called increasingly into question because of:

(a) the expansion of the ENCLOSURE of common land;

(b) the inability of commoners' associations to control stock levels in some areas.

New legislation has recently been set before parliament to give certain rights of land management to commoners which should effectively help to control these problems which often vary from area to area within Dartmoor. In some places overgrazing has resulted from a dramatic increase in stock numbers due to government and EEC incentives, in others undergrazing has caused the gradual return of grazing land on some commons to moorland . The need for pasture, its improvement, ploughing of land, enclosure and burning all continue to contribute to the changes in the Dartmoor landscape which now go ahead more rapidly than ever before.

1. a) With reference to Fig. 2.1. identify at least two other large areas of igneous rock outside south-west England.
   b) Suggest how these large areas of igneous rock could have formed.

2. What does the high density of surface drainage and extensive areas of blanket bog on Dartmoor suggest about the nature of igneous rocks such as granite?

3. Compile your own brief checklist of Dartmoor's physical features using a copy of the table below. (Refer to Fig. 2.3 and 2.4)

	Central area	Fringes
Relief		
Drainage		
Vegetation		

4. a) Which physical difficulties are likely to have placed severe restrictions on Dartmoor's agriculture?
   b) Explain why hill farming and stock rearing are best suited to Dartmoor's environment.

5. Describe the reasons for the use of burning as a system of land management on heather moors, and suggest any problems which might result.

Settlement Away from its fringes, the moor is still littered with prehistoric remains, testimony to the fact that they were built out of granite and that relatively little settlement has taken place in these areas since. The few settlements which did grow up in Dartmoor's interior were originally established to serve the needs of the farming communities. More recent developments have been concentrated around the periphery of the moor, especially along its southern edge, where the major north-east/south-west route runs to and from Plymouth (Fig. 2.5). Most of Dartmoor's settlements now cater for a much more diverse populace than the original villages. These places now fulfil a number of functions. For example, they act as dormitory settlements for people who commute or work elsewhere during the week, they may provide retirement havens for people seeking to live in a peaceful rural setting, and they provide holiday accommodation of various kinds, all in addition to being low-order service centres. As a

result of these changes many villages now have a much higher proportion of older people who, when they arrive at first, are normally still active, have their own cars, and make few demands on most types of service. As they grow older, they make increasing demands on medical services in particular, which local authorities in areas of sparse population such as Dartmoor often have difficulty in providing because of the high cost. At the 1981 census 23.3% of Dartmoor residents were of pensionable age (in comparison with 17.7% in Great Britain as a whole) and the number of people resident in homes for the disabled had risen dramatically from 47 in 1971 to 350 in 1981. Between 1971 and 1981 the population living on Dartmoor rose by 10%, the first increase after a long period of decline (Fig. 2.7). To house this

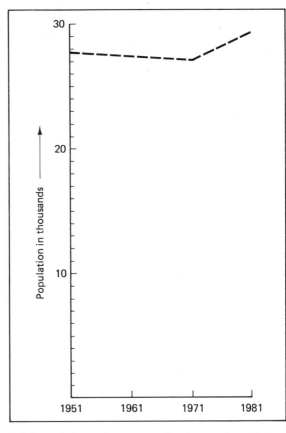

2.7 Population change on Dartmoor (population resident within National Park boundary)

increased population, the National Park Authority has sought to encourage the development of certain 'key' settlements. These have been selected partly to allow for more economic provision of certain aspects of

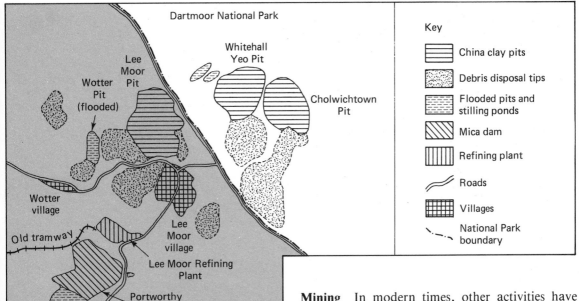

2.8 Lee Moor area of Dartmoor: china clay developments to 1977

INFRASTRUCTURE, but also to cater for demand for dormitory housing in areas popular with commuters. As only 35% of all employed people who live on Dartmoor actually work there as well, commuters form a very significant proportion of the economically active population. Where new housing has been built, care has been taken to limit the size of new estates, so that they do not 'swamp' existing communities and to ensure that these houses are not totally out of character with the existing ones and do 'blend in' to the local townscape.

6. Write a short essay on the following topic: 'The changing functions of settlement on Dartmoor.'

7. Why is the problem of ageing population of such concern in the more remote settlements?

8. Suggest what measures might be taken to make more modern housing 'blend in' to older settlements and explain why this is so important.

Mining In modern times, other activities have made a considerable impact on the Dartmoor landscape. One of these, mining, owes its existence to the intrusion of vapours associated with igneous activity into the granite batholith and its surrounding aureole while it was still hot. The presence of these minerals has contributed to the economy of Dartmoor at various times in the past. Tin mining has taken place since the twelfth century and copper, lead and iron ore were mined during the nineteenth century. All of these mine workings were on a fairly small scale and have long since been assimilated into the Dartmoor landscape.

The mining of china clay began on a similarly small scale early last century but has expanded during the twentieth century into a very large scale, highly mechanised, open cast operation. It now covers an extensive area in the Lee Moor district, straddling part of the southern boundary of the National Park and is presently being extended still further following a public enquiry in 1971 and decision to go ahead in 1972 (Fig. 2.8 and 2.9). Despite recent attempts at landscaping, the huge waste tips (Fig. 2.10) in this area still constitute a considerable visual intrusion on Dartmoor's scenery, a fact recognised in the following quotations from the *National Park Plan* published in 1977:

'It is the scale of the operation, and its destructive characteristics that cause real concern in the National Park today.'

'The N.P.A. regards the scale of current extraction operations as their major drawback on the landscape.'

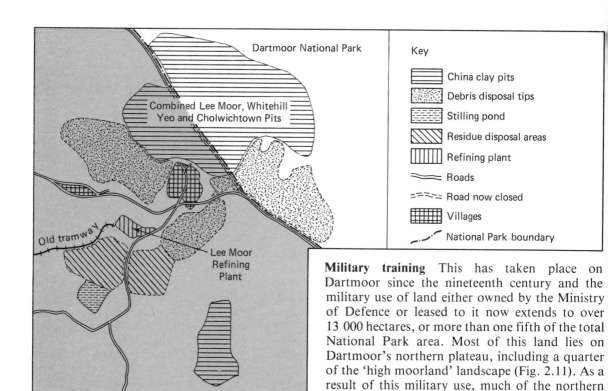

Key

China clay pits	
Debris disposal tips	
Stilling pond	
Residue disposal areas	
Refining plant	
Roads	
Road now closed	
Villages	
National Park boundary	

2.9 Lee Moor area of Dartmoor: future china clay developments

Military training This has taken place on Dartmoor since the nineteenth century and the military use of land either owned by the Ministry of Defence or leased to it now extends to over 13 000 hectares, or more than one fifth of the total National Park area. Most of this land lies on Dartmoor's northern plateau, including a quarter of the 'high moorland' landscape (Fig. 2.11). As a result of this military use, much of the northern plateau now has a network of tracks and because firing takes place regularly, the public is excluded for long periods of time. In many ways the use of land on Dartmoor for military training seems completely incompatible with its designation as a

2.10 China clay tips, Dartmoor

National Park, a fact recognised in a 'basic policy objective' of the National Park Committee in 1981: '.....military training in Dartmoor as a National Park is inappropriate. The objective must be its ultimate withdrawal.'

This incompatability was recognised initially by the National Trust who decided to discontinue permitting the Ministry of Defence to use an area of their land in the Ringmoor area (Fig. 2.11) for military training. The immediate response of the M.O.D. was to negotiate the use of an area of land belonging to the South-West Regional Water Authority in the Cramber Tor area (Fig. 2.11) on a two year trial basis, as at the time no less damaging location could be found. Ironically, this land lay even further into the southern moorland and had not previously been used as a training ground by the armed services! Pressure remains on the M.O.D. to meet their training needs elsewhere as the two year trial period has now expired and the National Park Committee has agreed to an extension for only one more year. However, a further setback to hopes of removing the military presence from the moor occurred in 1983 when the government approved a scheme to modernise the firing ranges at Willsworthy.

9. Refer to Fig. 2.8 and the photograph of the china clay waste tips Fig. 2.10. Describe the environment within which the residents of Lee Moor and Wotter villages must live.

10. Suggest which groups would have been likely to argue in favour of the expansion of the china extraction at Lee Moor at the 1971 public enquiry.

11. Why is the extraction of china clay today of much greater concern than the mining for metal ores which took place last century?

12. Study the areas shown on Fig. 2.12 and compare these with the military training areas shown on Fig. 2.11. Comment on your observations.

Water supply Another issue which has given rise to considerable controversy on Dartmoor during this century has been the construction of reservoirs for water storage and extraction. Having a fairly high rainfall, relatively deep valleys which are not difficult to dam, and providing the upper catchment areas for several of the south-west's major rivers, Dartmoor has been the inevitable, but sometimes unwilling victim of the South West Water Authority's attentions in attempting to satisfy increasing demands for water in the region. As Dartmoor escaped the direct effects of glaciation, it has almost a complete dearth of natural lakes and the eight reservoirs (Fig. 2.5) which are now to be found there have all been artificially created. The first of these, at Burrator and Holne Moor, were constructed as early as the 1890s to serve the needs of Plymouth and Paignton respectively. Since then six others have been built but none has given rise to more

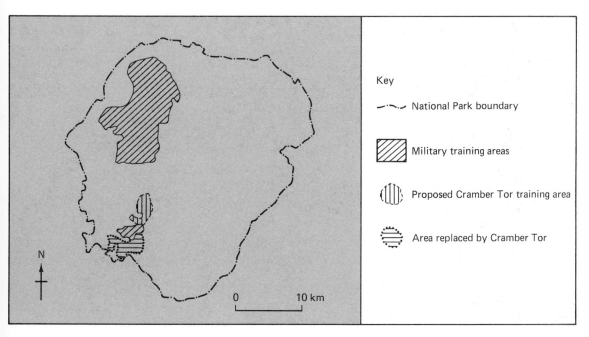

Key

⌐·⌐·⌐ National Park boundary

▨ Military training areas

⟨▥⟩ Proposed Cramber Tor training area

⌇ Area replaced by Cramber Tor

N

0   10 km

2.11 Military training areas on Dartmoor

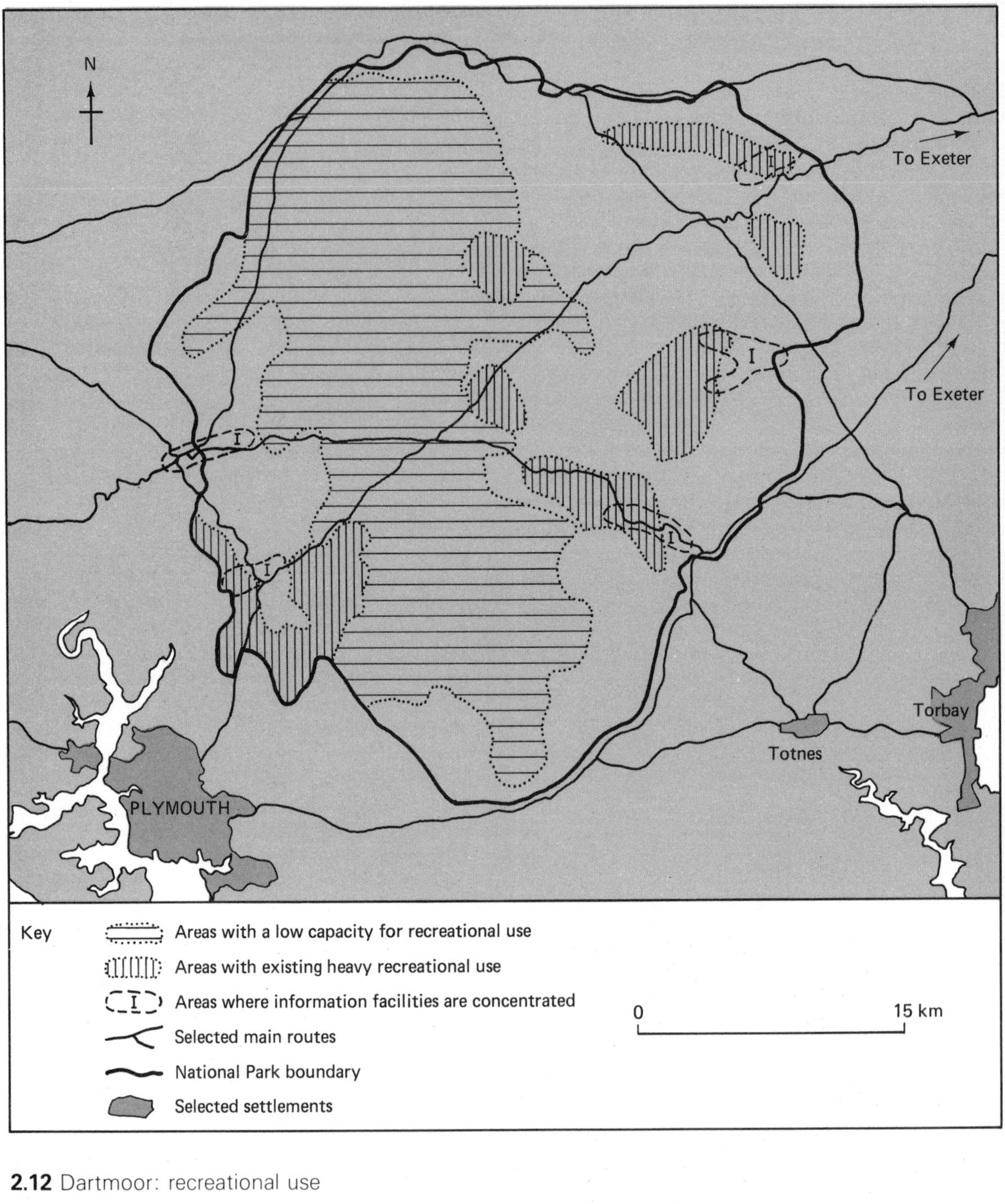
N
To Exeter
To Exeter
I
PLYMOUTH
Totnes
Torbay
Key
Areas with a low capacity for recreational use
Areas with existing heavy recreational use
Areas where information facilities are concentrated
Selected main routes
National Park boundary
Selected settlements
0
15 km

2.12 Dartmoor: recreational use

heated controversy than the Meldon Gorge scheme, which went to a public enquiry in 1965, and the proposal to use Swincombe which led to a similar enquiry in 1970. Eventually, the Meldon Reservoir, situated in a rocky chasm in north-west Dartmoor, was given the approval of the Secretary of State for the Environment and went ahead. The Swincombe scheme, proposed for one of the most beautiful valleys in central Dartmoor was rejected after violent objections from many individuals and organisations. Since that original threat to Swincombe, a further one arose in the late 1970s when a public inquiry was held over the building of a new reservoir at Roadford, near Launceston, outside the National Park. The threat was lifted when the Roadford scheme was approved, but if it had been rejected, Swincombe was one of the alternative sites being suggested.

Road scheme To the south of Okehampton, (Fig. 2.5) on the northern edge of Dartmoor and just within the National Park, lies one of the gorges most renowned for its wooded beauty. One of three proposals put forward in the latter half of the 1970s to by-pass Okehampton, and so remove one of the remaining bottlenecks on the A30 trunk road to the south-west, was to route the new road to the south of the town, cutting through the edge of the National Park, and spanning the splendid Okement Gorge with a massive new bridge. The other two alternatives both routed the new road through prime agricultural land to the north of the town. Again, a public inquiry was necessary to allow the various lobbies to put their cases for and against the three proposed routes. After considering the findings of the reporter, the Secretary of State for the Environment decided that the southern route should proceed, effectively destroying the peace and solitude of Okement Gorge, and many of its trees.

13. Why have so many reservoirs been created on Dartmoor during the past 100 years?

14. List some of the objections likely to have been made to the southern route proposal for the Okehampton by-pass by the conservation lobby.

Recreation While the impact of china clay mining, military training, and water abstraction on the Dartmoor landscape has been considerable, they have also been restricted to specific, sometimes fairly large, areas. Recreational demands, on the other hand, are much more diverse and this has led to the identification of zones (Fig. 2.12) of:
(a) low capacity for recreational use
(b) existing heavy recreational use.

The areas with low capacity for recreational use tend to lie within the least accessible parts of the moor where publicity which attracted large numbers of visitors would be to the detriment of the environment. Elsewhere, along the access roads and in the areas with existing heavy recreational use, extensive information (Fig. 2.12) and other tourist facilities are to be found. Most of Dartmoor's eight million annual visits take place within these areas, two thirds of which are made by Devonians themselves. One of the most popular 'honeypot' areas for these visitors lies around Haytor and the village of Widecombe

where the number of people who walk along the banks of the River Dart has necessitated recent restoration work. In order to better plan future recreational use the local planning authority, Dartmoor National Park, is to be provided with powers to establish and regulate visitors access to common land, thus preventing further 'scarring' of attractive areas and the resultant agriculture-recreation conflict. The fight may not yet be over, however, as the Dartmoor Preservation Association intend to take the decision to higher courts, and perhaps even to the House of Lords for final legal judgement if necessary.

Dartmoor Preservation Association (D.P.A.) The D.P.A. is one of the oldest and most well known local conservation and amenity pressure groups in Britain and celebrated its centenary in 1983. It began as a response to the enclosure of land and threats to commoners' rights in the 1880s and has sought to protect and enhance the Dartmoor landscape ever since. Various notable victories have been won in its battles against development, but even on the occasions when these have apparently been lost, concessions have been gained in the best interests of all. For more than a century the Association has acted as a check on the development of Dartmoor and has acquired a formidable reputation as a well-informed pressure group.

Increasing recreational pressure on Dartmoor's existing land-uses (Fig. 2.13) was only one of the

Open Moorland	52%
Enclosed farmland	35%
Forests and Woodland	9%
Urban/other uses	4%

2.13 Land-use on Dartmoor

reasons for the largest area of high moorland landscape in southern Britain being designated as a National Park in 1951. Since then, the pressures on the Dartmoor landscape have undoubtedly increased, but the National Park Authority, with the aid of its planning controls, is now better able to reconcile them.

15. Outline what you think the primary objectives of local conservation groups such as the Dartmoor Preservation Association are likely to be.

16. Suggest why the identification of the two distinct zones shown on Fig. 2.12 is likely to aid planners in provision for future recreation.

3
Sedimentary landscapes

Once a crust of igneous rocks had formed in Britain, they were subjected to weathering and erosion. Sediments were transported and deposited in rivers, lakes and seas and, as this material accumulated, it became compressed into SEDIMENTARY ROCKS. During the Alpine mountain building period, some 30 million years ago, these layers of rock were upfolded. Some stand out from the surrounding countryside as ESCARPMENTS or CUESTAS, with two types of LIMESTONE forming the most prominent of these scarp lines. Fig.3.1 shows the extent of the JURASSIC LIMESTONE belt, extending from the Cleveland Hills in North Yorkshire, through the Cotswolds and into the Purbeck Hills of Dorset. These rocks are yellow-brown in colour and not very resistant to weathering and erosion. Nevertheless, they still produce prominent scarp slopes, of up to 300 metres in the case of the Cotswolds

Much more widely distributed throughout the country are the younger escarpments of chalk, a white limestone made up almost entirely of calcium carbonate. The chalklands are shown in Fig. 3.2 and form a long series of upland ridges with smooth, rounded relief and scarp crests reaching to over 250 metres. The chalk extends from East Anglia and the Chilterns, through Salisbury Plain to Dorset. To the north lie the WOLDS of Lincolnshire and Yorkshire, and to the south the chalk dips below the London Basin reappearing as the North and South DOWNS.

Fig. 3.1 also shows the outcrops of grey CARBONIFEROUS or MOUNTAIN LIMESTONE, sometimes known as KARST scenery. These older limestones were often overlain with other sedimentary rocks and, where they are exposed, form uplands where the relief is more rugged and higher than in the areas of chalk and jurassic limestone, reaching heights of over 600 metres in some parts of the northern Pennines.

All of these sedimentary rocks have developed distinctive landscape features due basically to the fact that calcium carbonate, the basis of limestone, is soluble in water. All three rock types are PERMEABLE — that is, they allow the downward passage of water, but they differ in structure. Jurassic and carboniferous limestones are hard and compact, but have clear-cut joints and cracks through which water can pass (i.e. they are PERVIOUS) and which are further dissolved by the CHEMICAL WEATHERING of rainwater, a weak form of carbonic acid. Chalk, in contrast, has a more coarsely-grained open texture allowing free passage of water through porespaces and is therefore a POROUS rock. Water is held in the innumerable pore spaces in the chalk and seeps away slowly. The upper level of saturated rock is called the WATER-TABLE.

1. Refer back to Fig. 1.2 (p.4) and use it to explain the processes of landscape change which resulted in the formation of sedimentary rocks. Suggest a final process to follow DEPOSITION.

2. Compare the distribution, relief and drainage characteristics of CHALK, JURASSIC LIMESTONE and MOUNTAIN LIMESTONE in the British Isles.

Characteristic features of chalk landscapes

The North and South Downs are the chalk remains of a huge upfold or ANTICLINE which once covered most of the Weald (Fig. 3.2). The centre of the anticline has been eroded away, leaving the underlying clays and sandstones exposed as The Weald, flanked by the prominent chalk escarpments of the North and South Downs. Here the rock strata have been tilted by earth movement and cuestas formed with steep scarp slopes, and more gentle back or dip slopes. Sometimes, as in Salisbury Plain, the chalk forms more extensive areas of gently undulating uplands. Throughout the chalklands, surface drainage is usually absent and there are many DRY VALLEYS, cut into the underlying rock by

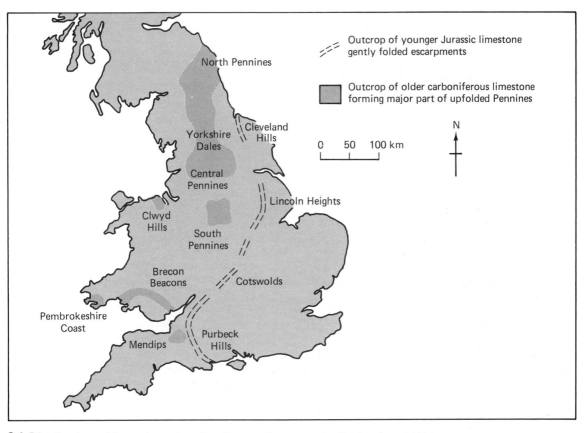

3.1 Distribution of jurassic and carboniferous limestone in England and Wales

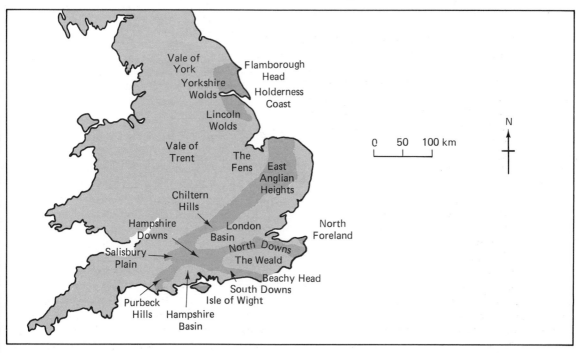

3.2 Distribution of chalklands of England

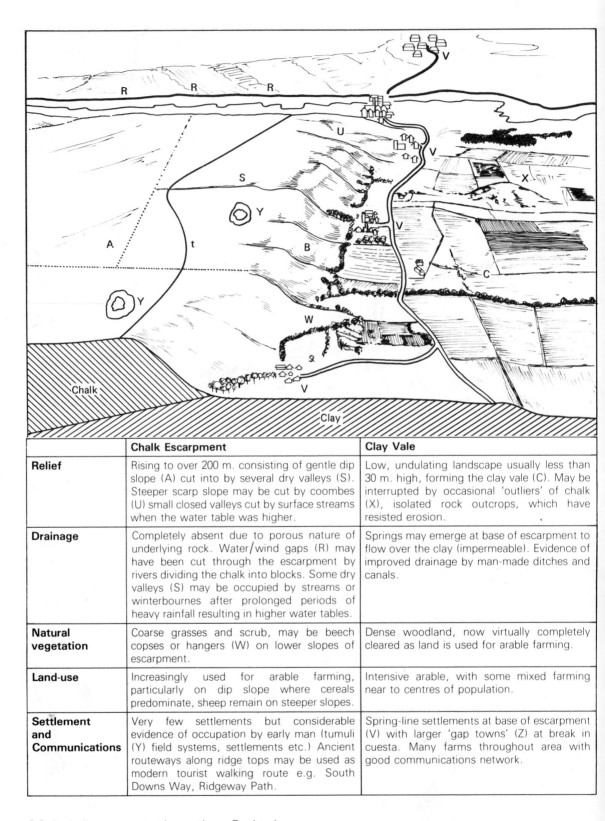

	Chalk Escarpment	Clay Vale
Relief	Rising to over 200 m. consisting of gentle dip slope (A) cut into by several dry valleys (S). Steeper scarp slope may be cut by coombes (U) small closed valleys cut by surface streams when the water table was higher.	Low, undulating landscape usually less than 30 m. high, forming the clay vale (C). May be interrupted by occasional 'outliers' of chalk (X), isolated rock outcrops, which have resisted erosion.
Drainage	Completely absent due to porous nature of underlying rock. Water/wind gaps (R) may have been cut through the escarpment by rivers dividing the chalk into blocks. Some dry valleys (S) may be occupied by streams or winterbournes after prolonged periods of heavy rainfall resulting in higher water tables.	Springs may emerge at base of escarpment to flow over the clay (impermeable). Evidence of improved drainage by man-made ditches and canals.
Natural vegetation	Coarse grasses and scrub, may be beech copses or hangers (W) on lower slopes of escarpment.	Dense woodland, now virtually completely cleared as land is used for arable farming.
Land-use	Increasingly used for arable farming, particularly on dip slope where cereals predominate, sheep remain on steeper slopes.	Intensive arable, with some mixed farming near to centres of population.
Settlement and Communications	Very few settlements but considerable evidence of occupation by early man (tumuli (Y) field systems, settlements etc.) Ancient routeways along ridge tops may be used as modern tourist walking route e.g. South Downs Way, Ridgeway Path.	Spring-line settlements at base of escarpment (V) with larger 'gap towns' (Z) at break in cuesta. Many farms throughout area with good communications network.

3.3 A chalk escarpment in southern England

3.4 Beachy Head

streams flowing when the water-table was higher than today, or possibly caused by surface erosion under PERIGLACIAL conditions when the rock was frozen and therefore impermeable. The main features of the chalk landscapes of southern England are summarised in Fig. 3.3. In those areas further north, the chalk may be deeply buried under more recent deposits, as in Lincolnshire and East Anglia where the rock has been covered with a mantle of glacial deposits. At several points around the coast, the chalk outcrops as impressive vertical cliffs and headlands such as Beachy Head (Fig. 3.4.), Dover and Flamborough Head. The permeability of the rock has enabled it to resist weathering very effectively, although at the base of the cliff, marine erosion is often very effective in causing the retreat of the cliff face.

3. Using Fig. 1.3 (p.5) together with Fig. 3.2, draw a simple annotated sketch section from the channel coast of southern England north to the London Basin, crossing North and South Downs and The Weald. Mark the main rocktypes on your section and the denuded Wealden anticline.

4. List out the landscape features shown on Fig. 3.3 and briefly explain their formation.

5. Describe and explain the differences in use of zones A, B and C on Fig. 3.3.

Changing land-uses in the chalk downlands:
A case study from Hampshire

The Hampshire Downs (Fig. 3.2) are located in central southern England and are a westward extension of the North and South Downs. The chalk upland (Fig. 3.5) is separated from the coast by a low-lying area, the Hampshire Basin, which has been infilled with younger tertiary rocks. Archaeological evidence suggests that the chalklands of southern England, including those of Hampshire, were the first areas in the British Isles to be farmed. This early use of the land involved the clearance of the original woodland cover during the Neolithic period to allow a combination of grain production and livestock rearing. The light, well-drained chalk soils were easily worked, unlike the heavier clays nearer the coast. Although the balance between grain and livestock production has varied considerably over the centuries, these two types of farming remain the basis of the local agricultural economy today. Change has come about by the introduction of much more intensive farming methods which have

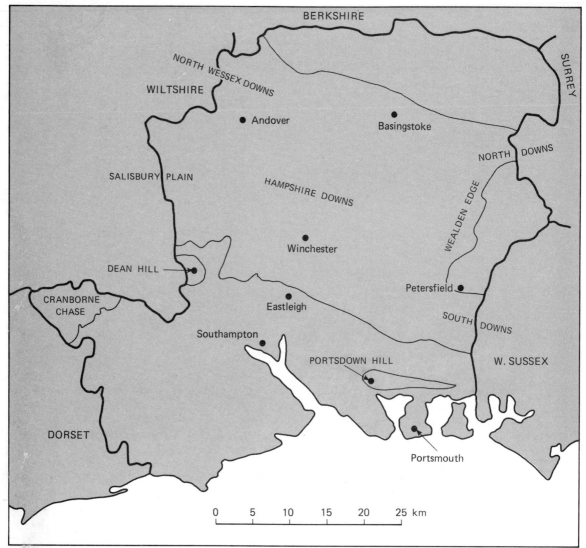

3.5 The Hampshire Basin

created a completely new agricultural landscape in this part of southern England.

The entry of the United Kingdom into the Common Market has had a significant impact on farming on Hampshire's chalklands. Farmers are given incentives to increase the area and yield of land under cereals. This assistance was set up to help small-scale farmers, especially those in southern France and Italy, but has resulted in the formation of 'grain mountains' from the already efficient farmers of southern England, northern France and Germany. Fig. 3.6 shows the increase in the area under wheat and barley between 1972 and 1982, in the chalkland area of Hampshire. The total area of these two crops has risen by over 8 000 hectares in the ten years, and the statistics

	Barley	Wheat
1972	54 351	22 611
1977	51 825	25 600
1982	44 946	40 084

3.6 Area of chalkland in Hampshire under wheat and barley (hectares)

also reveal a substantial decline in barley production, which has been more than compensated for by the increased production of wheat. This changing pattern is the result of numerous factors, including a drop in beer consumption, and rising oil prices which make it expensive to keep store cattle inside during the winter, fed on barley. At the same time, the recent development of spring-sown wheats has proved popular with farmers and has achieved high yields during the late 1970s and early 1980s when there were a number of very wet springs.

Despite the rise in cereal production in the Hampshire Downlands, the number of farms in the area which concentrate on wheat and barley production has not increased. This can be explained by both higher yields and by the continuing trend towards farm amalgamations (Fig. 3.7). This reduction in the number of farm units is only due to 'urban fringe' developments in a few instances, mostly around Andover and Basingstoke, it relates almost entirely to the continued search for efficiency in farming, which is resulting in much larger working units.

1972	1592
1977	1408
1982	1387

3.7 Total farm units in the Hampshire chalklands

The agriculture of this part of Hampshire is amongst the most organised and efficient in Britain. Most of the land is of Grade 3 quality — around the national average, so this productivity has not resulted from the land's intrinsic quality. It is related to the ease with which the soils can be worked, to the ability to use efficient machinery on large fields, and continued capital investments. Much of Hampshire's chalklands is in the hands of a few major companies, rather than traditional farmers. These companies include major supermarket groups, insurance companies and pension funds which tend to take rather less interest in the landscape which their 'agri-businesses' create.

The search for efficiency has been reflected in the loss of many farming units as they become merged, and by the grubbing up of hedgerows, clearing of trees and woodlands, draining marshlands and ploughing up the original downlands, thereby increasing the area of farmland. The average size of holding has increased by about 20% during the last ten years, as shown in Fig. 3.8. At the same time, the proportion of large farms within the chalk downlands has risen from about 26% to over 31% over the same ten year period.

Increasingly, Hampshire, like the chalk areas of East Anglia (Fig. 3.2) is taking on the appearance

	Total farmed area	Average farm size*
1972	157 389	98.9
1977	161 438	114.7
1982	161 406	116.4

*These farm sizes compare with an average of 53.7 ha in England and Wales, and 18.7 ha. in the EEC.

3.8 Hampshire chalklands: area farmed (hectares)

of a prairie landscape dominated in summer by fields of swaying corn. In August these fields are denuded by combine harvesters seemingly all in the same fortnight. They are then burnt to remove the straw (Fig. 3.9), or at least the stubble. This process, it is argued, returns plant nutrients to the soil as quickly as possible. Conservationists, on the other hand, would counter that burning actually kills off soil organisms necessary for healthy plant growth and, if uncontrolled, destroys the surrounding hedgerows and verges. Immediately after the fields have been burned, they are ploughed in preparation for the next year's crop. There is no need for rotations. The use of artificial fertilizers and herbicides allow grain to be grown in the same field year after year, and with guaranteed prices for their crop from the EEC, farmers make good use of the Common Agricultural Policy.

In view of the ease of cereal production, and associated financial advantages, it is perhaps surprising that recent years have also seen a rapid expansion of livestock rearing in the Hampshire chalklands.

Although numbers of cattle have increased, it is sheep rearing which has shown the greatest growth (Fig. 3.10), with an increase of some 70% over the ten years. As with changes in cereal production, the rise in sheep numbers can be attributed almost

1972	74 131
1977	98 332
1982	124 715

3.10 Hampshire chalklands: total sheep numbers

entirely to the EEC. Since Britain's entry, imports of New Zealand lamb have been greatly reduced, and sizeable grants and incentives are available from the Common Market for the production of 'sheepmeat'.

Unless there is a move by France to reduce British lamb production, it is likely that sheep numbers on the Hampshire chalklands will continue to rise — even more steeply if subsidies for grain production are stopped.

The Hampshire Downs have had so much capital investment, and are so safe from development being protected by strong planning policies, that the strength of local agriculture is assured. Hopefully, there will remain a place for the traditional downland features, the hill-top copse, old trackways, herb-rich chalk grassland and the riverside meadows, within the framework of capital intensive agriculture. Mechanisation has been carried to such a level that it is unlikely that there will be any further significant reduction in manning levels. Indeed, agriculture may soon be resulting in increased employment with the development of 'agric-industrial' complexes such as grain stores to serve co-operative ventures, freezing plant to cope with the increasing pea and bean industry, and processing plant for oil seed rape. This last crop has only recently come to Hampshire, but production is increasing. Presently much of the British crop is processed abroad into margarine and cattle feed, but there is likely to be demand for such processing to be carried out in Britain in the future.

6. Why did people initially use the Hampshire chalk downlands for farming, rather than the lower lying clay vales?

7. Describe and explain fully the changes which have taken place in farming on the Hampshire chalk downlands during the period since 1972. Use Figs. 3.6 -3.10 to help you.

8. Outline in what ways these changes have afffected the LANDSCAPE of the downlands.

9. Suggest what changes are anticipated in the local farming economy in the near future.

Characteristic features of mountain limestone landscapes

The most extensive area of carboniferous or mountain limestone in Britain occurs in the Pennines of northern England where the limestone blocks form upland areas which are separated by flat-floored and steep-sided valleys or 'dales'. The limestone has produced particularly striking landscape features which are summarised in Fig. 3.11. The surface of the hills is dry, with streams disappearing into SWALLOW HOLES or SINKS

3.9 Stubble burning in Hampshire

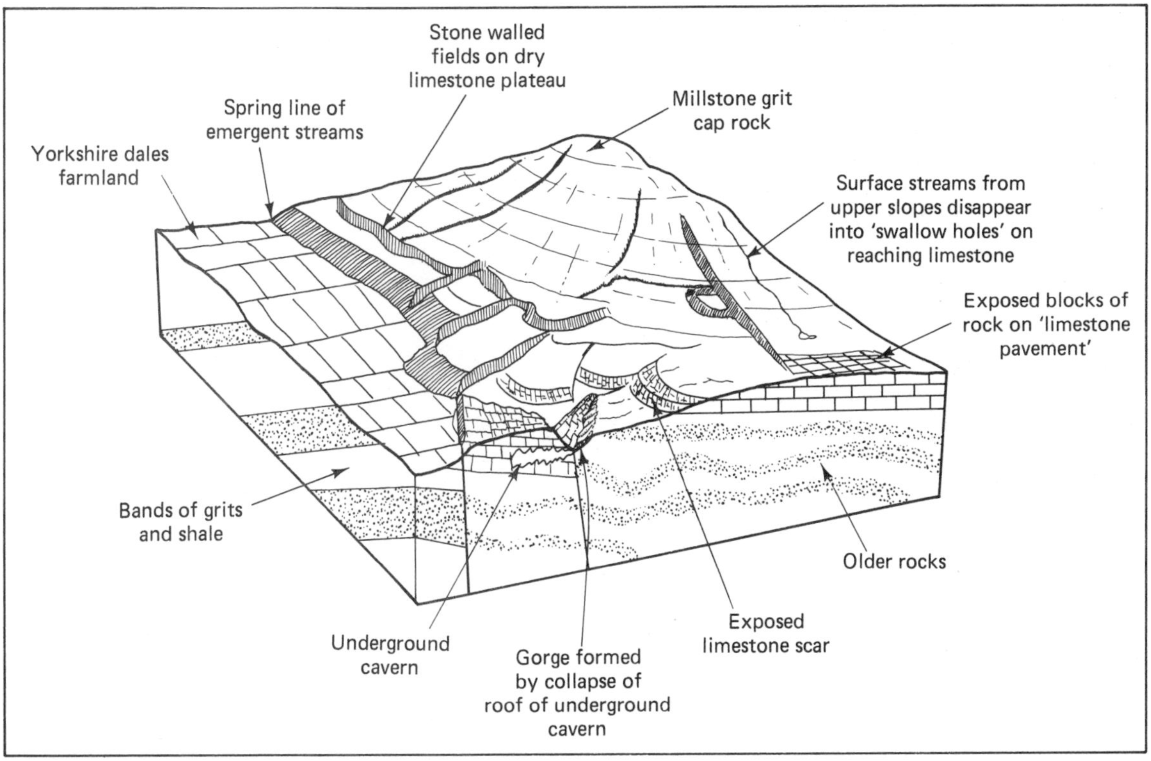
Stone walled
fields on dry
limestone plateau
Millstone grit
cap rock
Spring line of
emergent streams
Yorkshire dales
farmland
Surface streams from
upper slopes disappear
into 'swallow holes' on
reaching limestone
Exposed blocks of
rock on 'limestone
pavement'
Bands of grits
and shale
Older rocks
Underground
cavern
Gorge formed
by collapse of
roof of underground
cavern
Exposed
limestone scar

3.11 Features of carboniferous limestone scenery

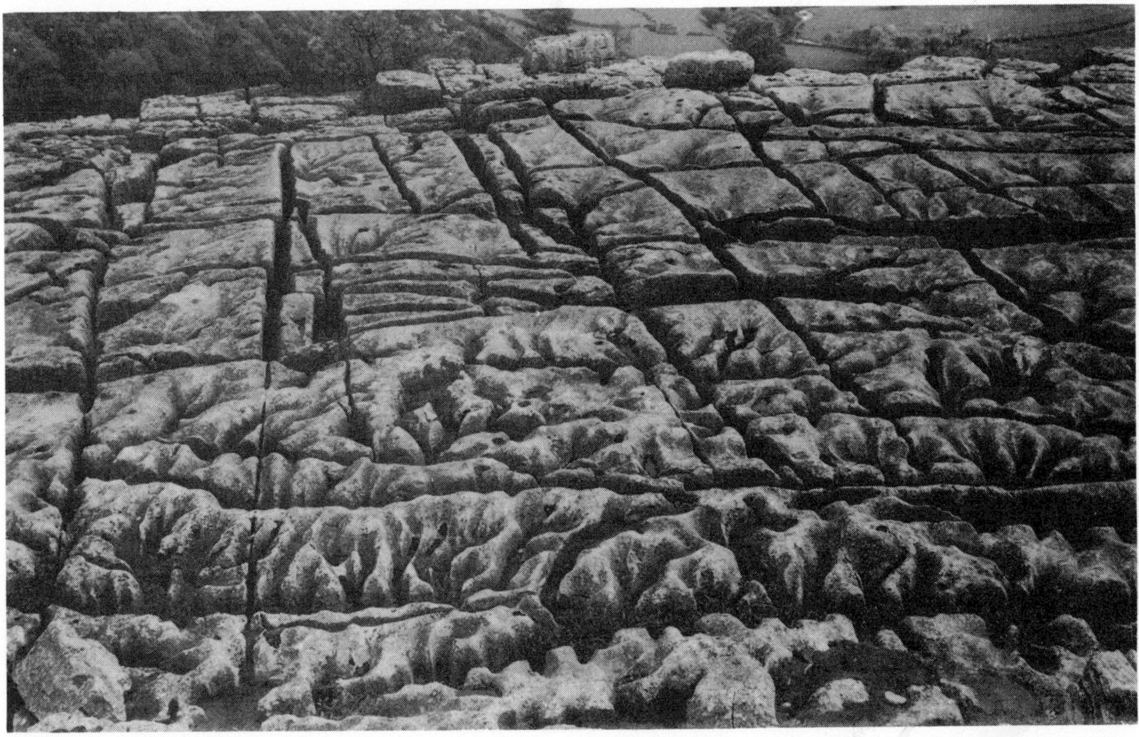

3.12 A limestone pavement in the Northern Pennines

on reaching the limestone, and much of the area is grass-covered moorland. In places, the thin soil cover has been easily eroded and the underlying rock exposed as LIMESTONE PAVEMENTS (Fig. 3.12). Here the well-developed joint system of the rock is clearly revealed as rainwater enlarges the joints or GRYKES, leaving behind 'bricks' of limestone or CLINTS. Occasionally, harder, more resistant strata within the limestone may be exposed on the sides of hills as prominent, cliff-like walls or LIMESTONE SCARS, (Fig. 3.11).

Despite these distinctive landscape features, perhaps even more impressive are those found underground in limestone areas. The natural drainage flowing down through the rock rather than over its surface, has created vast networks of pot-holes, caves and underground passageways which are typical features of the solutional erosion of mountain limestone.

The Ingleborough area of North Yorkshire, the Peak District of the south Pennines and the Mendip Hills (Fig. 3.1) all show spectacular examples of underground limestone scenery. Cheddar Gorge (Fig. 3.13) in the Mendips, is thought to have been formed by the collapse of the roofs of a series of underground limestone caverns. Where the limestone is underlain by an impermeable rock such as clay, grit or shale, the underground water may issue as a spring near the base of the limestone, restoring surface drainage such as in the Mendips where the River Axe flows out strongly from Wookey Hole.

10. List the main landscape features shown on Fig. 3.11 and explain their formation.

Land use in the Northern Pennines: The Yorkshire Dales National Park

The carboniferous limestone uplands of the northern Pennines are one of the most sparsely populated parts of England. The lack of surface drainage and water supplies have combined with poor communications to limit settlement. Farming is the main land-use, but even here, the thin soils and higher rainfall of these areas effectively eliminate arable farming and limit the farmer's options considerably with the open moorland providing poor pasture suitable only for sheep rearing, although cattle are grazed on the lower slopes and in the dales. Despite these physical

3.13 Cheddar Gorge

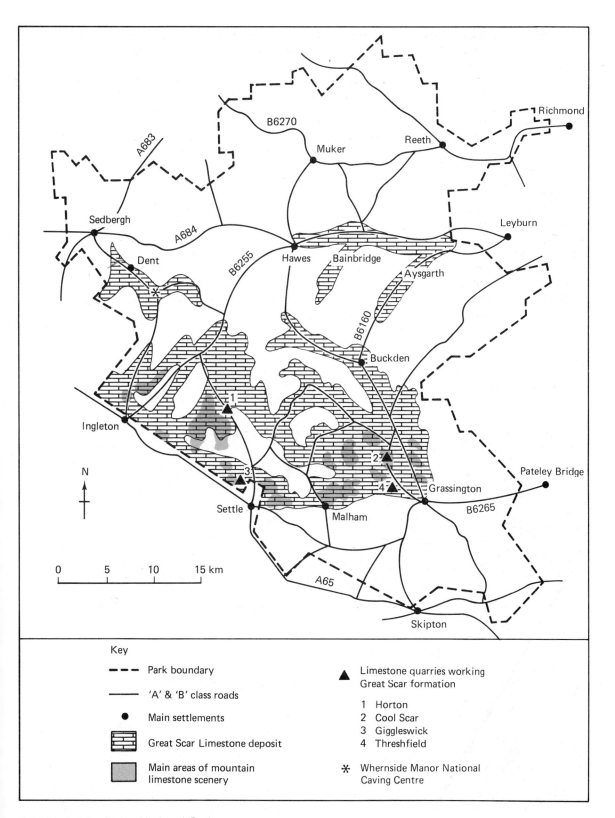

Key

- – – – Park boundary
- ——— 'A' & 'B' class roads
- ● Main settlements
- Great Scar Limestone deposit
- Main areas of mountain limestone scenery

▲ Limestone quarries working Great Scar formation

1 Horton
2 Cool Scar
3 Giggleswick
4 Threshfield

✳ Whernside Manor National Caving Centre

3.14 Yorkshire Dales National Park

3.15 A limestone quarry in the Yorkshire Dales National Park

limitations, as in the chalklands of the south, the past decade has seen land and livestock being more intensively managed. In the dales this has resulted in large new farm buildings appearing, in modern materials, to supercede the traditional system of wintering animals in the dispersed stone field barns so characteristic of the area. Farm amalgamations have led to the lack of maintenance of the distinctive dry stone walls. In the Yorkshire Dales National Park (Fig. 3.14) the management committee have taken special action to provide resources to encourage farmers to retain these features which are regarded as 'distinctive elements of the cultural heritage and landscape character of the Dales'.

Limestone quarrying is a long-established activity in the Dales with, in the past, many small quarries serving local need for building materials, including the stone barns and walls referred to above. In the post-war period, however, there has been rapid escalation in the rate of limestone extraction associated with the steel making, cement, chemical and glass making industries as well as use in sugar refining and agriculture. The National Park Authority is concerned about the effects of increased extraction of limestone for several reasons. Firstly, four of the five quarries currently operating are based in the south-western part of the National Park where the massive Great Scar Limestone (Fig. 3.14) is several hundred metres thick and is responsible for much of the landscape quality of this part of the Park. The limestone is of high chemical purity, with the calcium carbonate content exceeding 95% over most of the area. Less than a quarter of the output from these quarries is used for purposes requiring limestone of this high quality with over 70% used for aggregate. The National Park Authority has argued that this is wasteful use of a finite resource.

The quarries are also criticised for their visual intrusion on the landscape (Fig. 3.15). The increased production affects the landscape character of the National Park and is seen as a particular threat to the underground cave systems and other features of geomorphological and scientific interest. Finally, the quarrying industry has tended to favour the flexibility offered by road transport for quarry products. The impact of such traffic, concentrated on certain minor roads in the National Park causes great concern. The use of

3.16 Damage to stalactite and stalagmite formations

larger vehicles, carrying loads of up to 24 tonnes, pose particular problems on the narrow winding roads with pressure from tourist bodies to restrict the movement of these loads, and from road hauliers to increase the maximum gross weight of vehicles to allow more economic transport of quarry products.

The National Park has the greatest concentration of limestone pavement (Fig. 3.12) in Britain with the area around Malham and Arncliffe providing the most extensive exposures. Although these sites are both visually distinctive and of considerable scientific interest, many lack effective protection with the clints removed by contractors for sale as rockery stone for use in town gardens! Even the underground cave systems are not protected from damage. The North Pennines Cave Area, which is centred on the National Park, contains more than 600 cave systems, more than in all the rest of England, which total over 320 km in length. At least 52 of these caves are considered to be of national importance and the area is visited by geologists, geomorphologists, biologists, archaeologists and hydrologists as well as recreational 'pot-holers'.

Apart from the threat from limestone quarrying, mentioned above, cavers themselves are responsible for the high level of erosion in some of the most popular cave systems by the collection of specimens and the destruction of rock formations such as STALACTITES and STALAGMITES in order to allow access into the caves (Fig. 3.16). These underground caverns are even threatened by pollution by the dumping of rubbish and even dead farm animals down potholes!

11. Suggest why large-scale commercial farming has not developed to the same extent in the mountain limestone areas of the northern Pennines as in the chalk downlands of southern England.

12. Outline those changes which HAVE taken place in farming in this area in recent years and suggest why these are causing some concern.

13. Describe in detail the main threats to the distinctive limestone scenery of the Yorkshire Dales National Park and suggest what measures might be taken to safeguard the area.

4
Glaciated Landscapes

On various occasions in the geological past, areas of Britain to the north of a line drawn approximately between the Bristol Channel and the Thames Estuary (Fig. 4.1) have been covered in ice, and the areas to the south of this line were affected by glacial outwash. At these times, due to a gradual but marked fall in average temperatures, permanent ice sheets formed and expanded in higher upland areas and these became the main centres for ice dispersal in the British Isles. (Fig. 4.1).

As a result of ice action, the highest of Britain's upland areas, the Scottish Highlands, the Lake District and Snowdonia, have all been etched with the characteristic features of glaciated highland landscapes (Figs. 4.2, 4.3). The lower lying areas of Britain were not exempt from the direct and indirect effects of these ice-sheets either, and many bear the remnants of extensive GLACIAL or FLUVIOGLACIAL deposition. (Figs. 4.2).

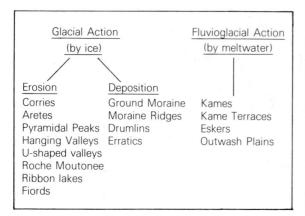

Glacial Action (by ice)		Fluvioglacial Action (by meltwater)
Erosion	**Deposition**	
Corries	Ground Moraine	Kames
Aretes	Moraine Ridges	Kame Terraces
Pyramidal Peaks	Drumlins	Eskers
Hanging Valleys	Erratics	Outwash Plains
U-shaped valleys		
Roche Moutonee		
Ribbon lakes		
Fiords		

4.2 Landscape features resulting from glacial and fluvioglacial action

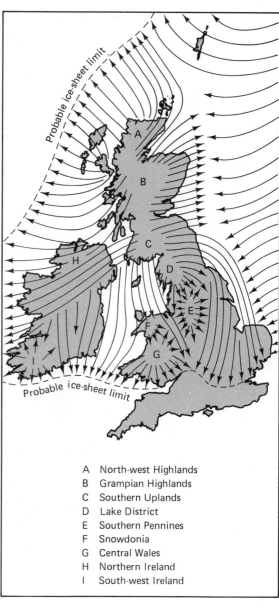

A North-west Highlands
B Grampian Highlands
C Southern Uplands
D Lake District
E Southern Pennines
F Snowdonia
G Central Wales
H Northern Ireland
I South-west Ireland

4.1 Ice movement and centres of ice dispersal in the British Isles

Case study of a glaciated highland landscape Snowdonia

Physical background The highest peak in England and Wales, Mount Snowdon, at 1085 metres (Fig. 4.4), lies at the heart of one of the major glaciated landscapes in the British Isles. Snowdonia as the region is known, provides some excellent examples of landforms resulting from HIGHLAND GLACIATION, but the origins of the rocks which are found there date back to times much earlier than the Ice Age, to the Pre-Cambrian period, some 600 million years ago.

The complex geology of Snowdonia (Fig. 4.5.) results from layers of IGNEOUS and SEDIMENTARY ROCK being uplifted and folded in the past. This provided a foundation of high, resistant igneous peaks, separated by wide valleys of softer sedimentary rocks which existed in pre-glacial times, and which were subjected to extensive glaciation on several occasions during the Pleistocene Period (Ice Age).

As a result of this repeated glacial advance and retreat, numerous classic features of highland glaciation are to be found. For example, around the PYRAMIDAL PEAK of Snowdon (Figs. 4.4, 4.6) a series of ARETES such as Bwlchysaethau and Crib-goch radiate outwards and form divisions betwen basin-shaped CWMS or CORRIES, the floors of which are often occupied by small lakes or TARNS such as Glaslyn, and littered with SCREE. To the north-east of Snowdon, a deep U-SHAPED VALLEY or GLACIAL TROUGH is found, the pass of Llanberis, with its MISFIT STREAM, the Afon Nant Peris. Similarly, to the south-east another u-shaped valley can be identified but here the valley floor is occupied by the Llyn Gwynant, a RIBBON LAKE, in addition to its misfit stream, the Afon Glaslyn. This misfit stream and ribbon lake are fed from the west by a series of streams which flow down from HANGING VALLEYS on the sides of Mount Snowdon. In the later stages of glaciation still further modification took place as a

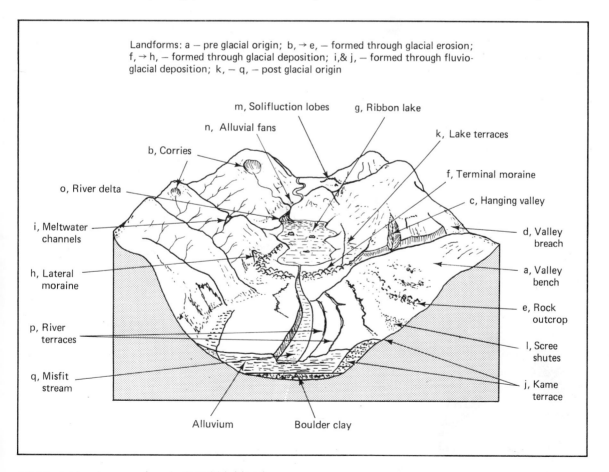

4.3 Model landscape of a glaciated highland

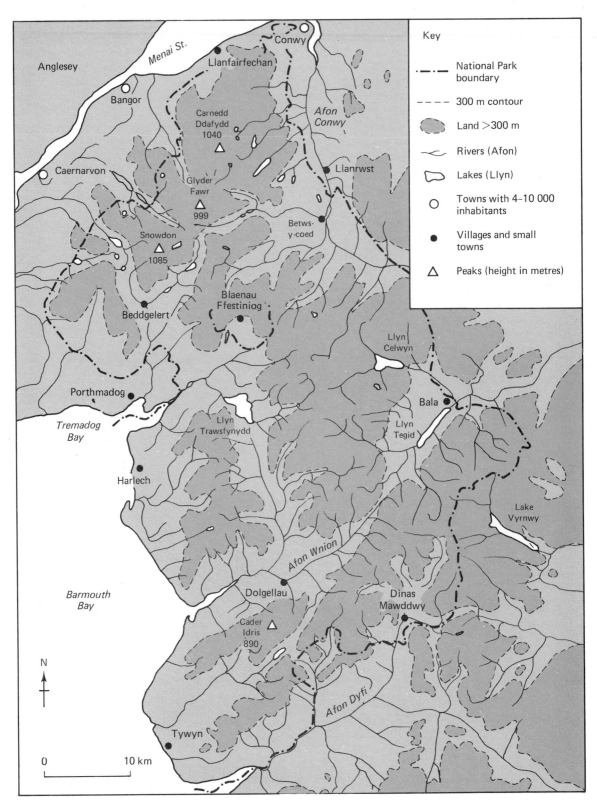

4.4 Snowdonia: upland, rivers and major settlements

result of SOLIFLUCTION or freeze-thaw processes which caused widespread landslip of remaining loose surface material on valley and mountain sides. Landscapes such as this are not just confined to one area of Snowdonia however. They are also to be found around Cader Idris and Tal-y-llyn and in the Glyder Fawr, Cwm Idwal and Nant Francon areas, (Fig. 4.4).

As in most upland areas of Britain relatively little true 'wildscape' remains in Snowdonia. The few remaining valleyside oakwoods in the west are now protected as they are the only remnants of natural forest left. Much of the rest of Snowdonia consists of grass moorland with bracken predominating on lower slopes. Some of this area is managed for grouse shooting purposes.

1. Explain why the higher upland areas (Fig. 4.1) were the main centres for ice dispersal in the British Isles.

2. Draw and annotate three cross-sections to illustrate valleys before, during and after glaciation.

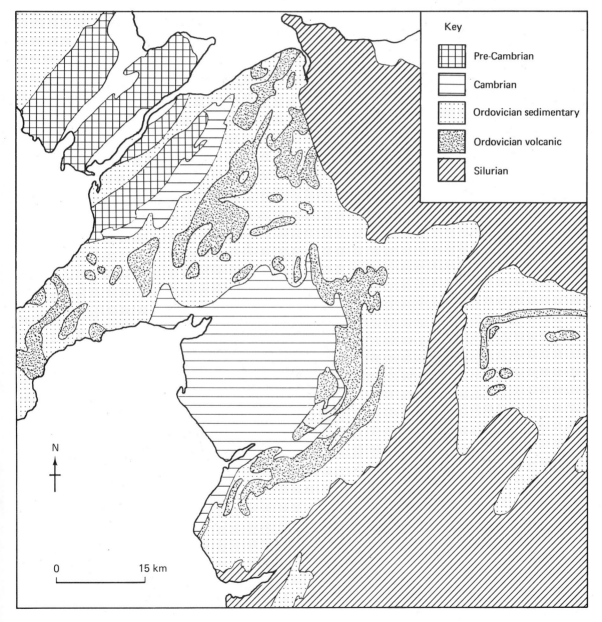

4.5 Simplified geological map of Snowdonia

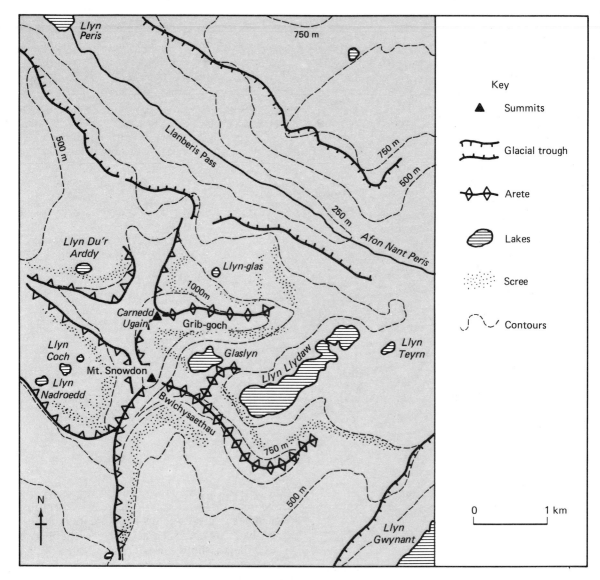

4.6 Mount Snowdon: classic features of highland glaciation

3. With the aid of a traced copy of the map (Fig. 4.6) of Mount Snowdon, label as many feature of highland glaciation as you can.

Farming and Forestry Human influence has created two contrasting farming zones within Snowdonia. The higher, inland area corresponds with the traditional perception of upland farming in Britain, concentrating on livestock, especially sheep and beef cattle production due to the constraints of the physical environment. In the past these farms typically had a small proportion of enclosed and improved INBYE land in comparison to open, unimproved, rough grazing higher up on the mountain sides. Increasingly, this proportion of improved land is getting even smaller as these farmers rely more and more on winter fodder being bought-in, or use over-wintering facilities elsewhere for their stock. In addition to this, the abandonment of the higher and more remote farms has led to reversion of previously improved land to rough grazing. As a means of making ends meet, some of these farmers in higher areas who are fortunate enough to own land near to the major tourist routes, have been diversifying into provision of camping and

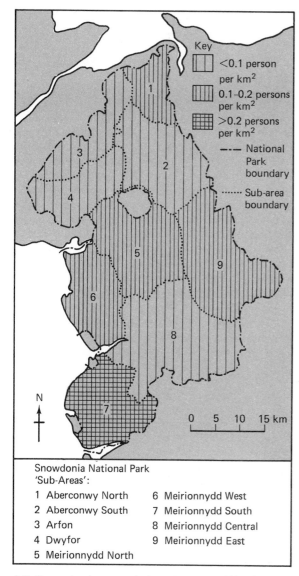

Key

	<0.1 person per km²
	0.1–0.2 persons per km²
	>0.2 persons per km²

— · — National Park boundary

········· Sub-area boundary

Snowdonia National Park 'Sub-Areas':

1 Aberconwy North
2 Aberconwy South
3 Arfon
4 Dwyfor
5 Meirionnydd North
6 Meirionnydd West
7 Meirionnydd South
8 Meirionnydd Central
9 Meirionnydd East

0 5 10 15 km

4.7 Snowdonia: population densities (1975)

Parks of England and Wales.

Population and settlement Snowdonia has always been relatively sparsely populated (Fig. 4.7) in comparison with other areas of England and Wales. There is no doubt that the rigours of the physical environment have discouraged people from settling there in the past and that remoteness and inaccessibility have also played a part. Today, some 25 000 people choose to live there and some indications suggest that net emigration, which saw Snowdonia's population fall by 16% between 1951 and 1971, is now no longer taking place on the same scale. Unfortunately, much of the out-migration which does still take place is of young people, and most of the incomers come from the retirement age-groups, producing a progressively ageing and imbalanced population structure (Fig. 4.8) in comparison to England and Wales as a

| | Percentage of total population | |
	Snowdonia	England and Wales
Age Group		
Under 15 years	21.7	25.0
Working age groups	56.8	59.1
Retirement age groups	21.5	15.9

4.8 Comparison of population structures of Snowdonia with England and Wales

whole. In addition, some redistribution of population within the area is also discernable, as depopulation continues in the interior, and an increase takes place around the coast. A major problem accompanies this movement. The smaller settlements in central Snowdonia are in danger of losing basic services such as primary schools and even village shops, especially in the more picturesque villages where houses have been bought up as 'second homes'.

The issue of SECOND HOME ownership gives rise to very strong feelings amongst many of the native inhabitants of Snowdonia, and indeed throughout Wales. The country as a whole is estimated to have 30 000 second homes, or approximately 15% of the British total. The houses in question are nearly always to be found in small rural settlements and because the incomers who buy up these houses can afford to pay very much more than young local people, this trend has contributed to depopulation. Furthermore, as the houses are only occupied for a fraction of the year, mostly in summer, this detracts from the sense of community in these small settlements. It is recognised that the buying up of derelict and decaying property was initially

caravan sites and bed and breakfast accommodation. On the lower farming zone, in the broader valleys and near to the coast more intensive dairy units are to be found, and others which operated in conjunction with the upland hill farms as one integrated working unit, despite their distance apart.

Another major component of landscape change during this century has been the very significant expansion in commercial, largely coniferous, forestry especially in the Gwydyr Forest and Coed Y Brenin areas. By 1980, the Forestry Commission owned 16% of the total area of Snowdonia, one of its largest representations in the ten National

beneficial but, as demand has continued to increase, and now far exceeds supply, market prices have soared and new building has taken place. All of this has changed the physical, cultural and social character of the more popular villages. Gwynedd County Council has formulated proposals to control the problem, including the abolition of domestic rate relief on holiday homes and the introduction of some form of licensing system, but both measures have been rejected by the government. Continued lack of success in tackling the problem and the strength of local feeling has provoked extreme reaction by a few, in setting fire to, or destroying, more than 80 second homes since December 1979 (Fig. 4.9).

4. Suggest why many of the higher, more remote farms have been abandoned.

5. Explain how certain higher and lower level farms have come to operate as a single unit.

6. Using Fig. 4.8 compare the population structure of Snowdonia with that of England and Wales as a whole.

7. Why do you think that the issue of second homes arouses such strong feelings amongst the native inhabitants of Snowdonia?

8. What measures can local planning authorities adopt to stem the spiral in second home ownership?

Mining and quarrying As far back as Roman times metals are thought to have been mined in Snowdonia. Copper, for example, was mined at one time to the east and west of Mount Snowdon and on the sides of the mountain itself. Both iron ore and manganese deposits have been exploited in the past and even panning for gold in Snowdonia's rivers is not unknown! As most of these mineral ores are relatively low grade, their exploitation has not proved economically viable in the recent past. This could change, however, as reserves elsewhere in the world become depleted, new technology is developed and with the availability of government aid or subsidies. The first signs of increasing interest in Snowdonia were seen in 1969 when the multi-national Rio Tinto Zinc company was found to have been buying up mineral exploitation rights and had been drilling for copper in the Capel Hermon area, without planning permission. As yet, no large scale mining developments have begun, but if they were proposed, they would be likely to be OPENCAST operations involving considerable visual landscape intrusion, without stringent safeguards. Such visual intrusion would not be new to Snowdonia as the rocks of the area have long been worked to produce roofing slate. At Blaenau Ffestiniog, in particular, an area in central Snowdonia, but specifically excluded from the National Park (Fig. 4.4), huge and unsightly slate quarries were to be found, employing large numbers of men. Since the mid 1970s, when some 350 hectares of derelict slate workings were identified in Snowdonia, considerable environmental rehabilitation has taken place with funding from the Welsh Development Agency. After

4.9 A fire-damaged 'second home' in Snowdonia

46

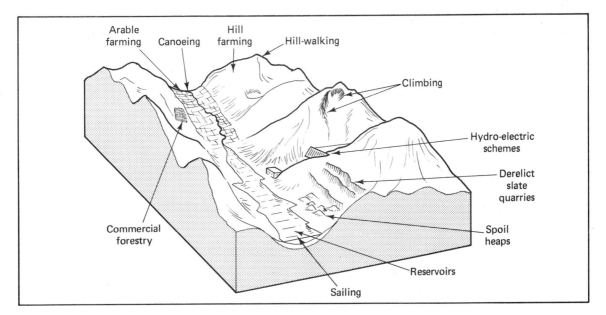

4.10 Use of the Snowdonian landscape

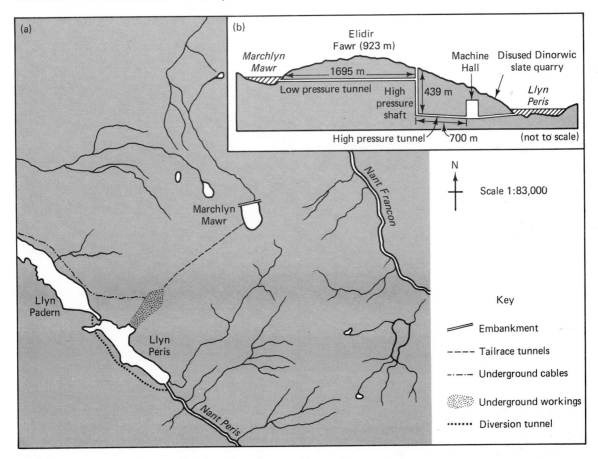

4.11 a) Dinorwic pumped storage scheme b) Cross-section to illustrate Dinorwic pumped storage scheme

extensive landscaping and some preservation work, part of the old quarries at Blaenau Ffestiniog have been opened up as a tourist attraction. they record for posterity the relics of an industry which is now all but extinct and employs very few people today.

Electricity production Glaciated highland areas such as Snowdonia also provide many advantages for the siting of hydro-electric power schemes (Fig. 4.10). These include:

(a) high mountains with steep slopes which provide fast flowing water;

(b) natural storage reservoirs in high cwms and deep ribbon lakes;

(c) narrow valleys which can be easily dammed;

(d) solid, often IMPERMEABLE rock which provides good foundations, and cuts down on water loss through seepage.

Each of these factors, combined with the area's relatively high rainfall, contributed to the development of several small hydro-electric power stations at the beginning of this century. These original stations were of the conventional type where water flows one-way through a power station, driving the turbines which in turn power the generators. More recently, two major 'pumped storage' schemes have been constructed at Ffestiniog (opened in 1963) and at Dinorwic (Figs. 4.11 a) and b)) which opened in 1983. In pumped storage schemes, water is allowed to flow

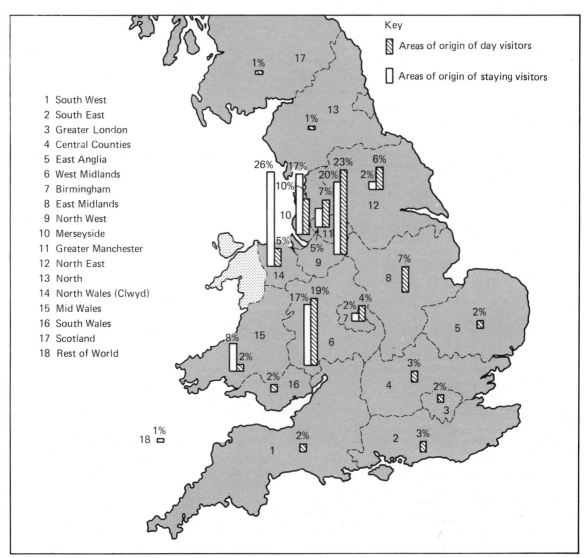

4.12 Areas of origin of day visitors and staying visitors to Gwynedd

down from a high level storage reservoir driving a turbine and generating electricity during daytime peak demands. At night, surplus electricity from base load thermal and nuclear power stations is used to pump water back up from a low level lake to the high level reservoir. The attraction of these schemes is that, although electricity cannot be stored in large quantities, water can, and is then used to produce power when required and virtually instantaneously. Elidir Fawr, the mountain where the Dinorwic scheme has been created was an ideal location because of the close proximity of the two lakes, Marchlyn Mawr, high up on the mountain, and Llyn Peris some 500 metres lower, at its foot. Although both of these lakes had to be extended slightly, neither involved the flooding of agricultural land, and the difference in altitude ensured a good 'head' of water (Figs 4.10, 4.11).

The availability of vast supplies of water was also a major reason behind the decision to locate Britain's first inland nuclear power station at Trawsfynydd in Snowdonia. There the large lake from which the power station takes its name provides 160 million litres of cooling water per hour for the plant before being slowly returned with the aid of a barrage designed to ensure that it has been cooled to almost the original temperature.

9. Contrast the effects on the landscape of (a) mining, (b) quarrying operations in the past.

10. With the aid of Fig. 4.9 assess human impact on a typical glaciated valley in Snowdonia.

11. Explain why so many hydro-electric power schemes are located in glaciated upland areas such as Snowdonia.

12. State reasons for the choice of Elidir Fawr as a site for a pumped-storage H.E.P. scheme and Trawsfynydd for a nuclear power station.

Tourism and recreation The dramatic glaciated landscape of Snowdonia, with its high mountains divided by deep glacial troughs (Fig. 4.10) also attracts millions of visitors each year. In 1980, the total number of day visitors was estimated to be 3.72 million and total staying visitors about 3.18 million! The maps and graphs showing the home areas of 'day' and 'staying' visitors (Fig. 4.12) clearly show that many were willing to travel considerable distances to sample the delights of Snowdonia, even if in some cases it was just for part of a day. The tables in Fig. 4.13 suggest that the majority of these visitors go there because of prior knowledge and to indulge in fairly passive forms of recreational activity.

a)

Scenery and Landscape	23%
Specific attractions	17%
Friends and relatives	14%
Outdoor activities	13%
Enjoyed previous visit	11%
Others	22%

b)

Enjoyed previous visit	24%
Friends/Relatives	15%
Scenery/Landscape	14%
Second Home	11%
Outdoor Activities	9%
Others	23%

4.13 a) Day visitors: main reason for trip to Gwynedd
b) Staying visitors: main reason for trip to Gwynedd

A significant minority, however, go there to participate in a wide range of very active outdoor pursuits — for which, glaciated uplands such as Snowdonia provide resources in abundance. Perhaps the most obvious of these is hill-walking, where the enthusiast can gain ample reward for strenuous efforts in reaching a peak, ridge or headland, with spectacular views over surrounding cwms, cliffs, mountains, lakes or the sea coast. The main routes for hillwalkers concentrate on the ascent of the fourteen peaks which are over about 900 metres in height in the north of Snowdonia, and on Cader Idris and the Aran range in the south. Climbers also find testing and difficult routes, especially in the north of the region, where the steep crags provide challenges for even the most expert. The snow and ice which can form on the north and east facing cliffs of these mountains in the early months of the year also attract more proficient climbers at that time. Yet another abundant resource in Snowdonia, previously referred to within the context of power production, is fast flowing water. This white water provides excitement and thrills for canoeists and recently saw Snowdonia's recognition as a centre of international status, when the world championships were held at Bala in 1982.

One consequence of the increasing popularity of Snowdonia's highland glaciated landscape for all kinds of fieldwork, as well as for active recreation,

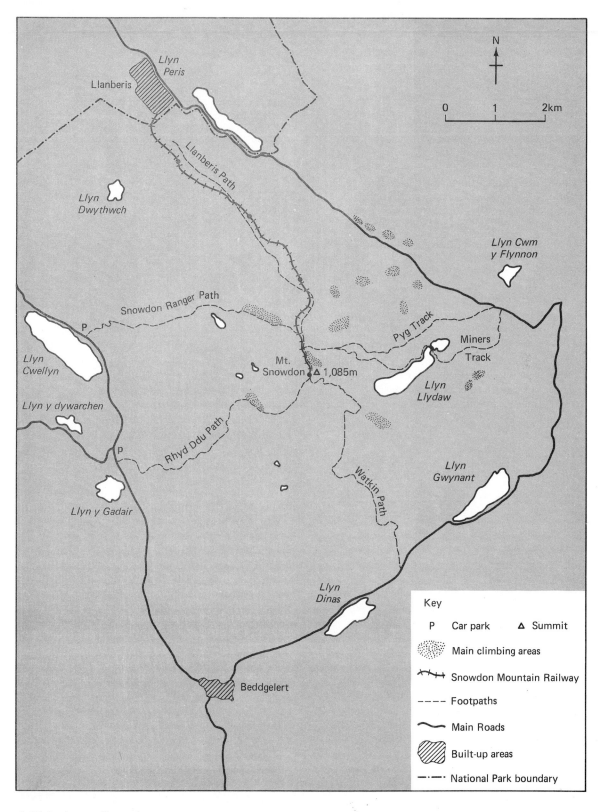

4.15 Paths on Snowdon

has been the proliferation of outdoor centres. In 1980, there were 138 centres within the National Park and an additional 110 within 15 km of the Park boundary. The outdoor pursuits previously described appeared to be amongst the most frequently undertaken by centre residents (Fig. 4.14). However, the cumulative effect of over-use by fieldwork groups of certain popular areas, has resulted in the need to initiate a 'rota of use' of such locations, and the banning of further outdoor centres by the National Park Authority.

Hillwalking	90%
Rock climbing	60%
Canoeing	55%
Pony trekking	24%
Orienteering	24%

4.14 Snowdonia: most frequent activities from outdoor centres

Outdoor centre residents make up only a very small proportion of the total number of visitors to Snowdonia, however, and probably contribute proportionally less damage to the landscape as most of their activities take place away from those areas where most tourists congregate. One of the most popular areas for most tourists, is on Mount Snowdon itself (Fig. 4.15) where the mountain is literally being worn away. The paths in the summit area in particular have been subject to considerable erosion over a prolonged period and this area has suffered most, largely because it was the ultimate destination for walkers, 10 000 of whom were recorded by footpath counters in 1980, and for travellers on the Snowdon Mountain Railway who numbered 72 000 that same year. The trampling effects of these hundreds of thousands of visitors have left a summit area which is virtually devoid of surface vegetation and covered in stones. A rather unsightly cluster of service buildings further spoils this area. Similar damage has taken place on the six different foot paths (Fig. 4.15) which eventually lead to the summit. Once erosion actually begins on these paths, it spreads very quickly due to the cumulative effects of trampling by thousands of pairs of boots (Figs. 4.15, 4.16), and the action of ice, rain and wind. At first, and especially in steep sections, the layer of plants which bind together the thin layer of soil is worn away. This exposed soil is then carried downslope by ice, rain and wind allowing the beginnings of a gully to form. As these gullies develop, the walkers, understandably, trudge along their sides in order to avoid these loose rocks and stones. In this way the erosion continues and the paths get progressively wider (to more than 12 metres at one point!) and more ugly.

Realisation of the deterioration taking place as a result of the increasing visitor numbers first occurred early in the 1970s and resulted in the Snowdon Management Scheme, which began in 1979. The first 5 year phase of this project sought to:

'(a) make good past neglect and minimise the effects of erosion caused largely by recreational use of the mountain;

(b) reduce the impact of visitor use on the mountain, on existing farmlands and fragile conservation areas;

(c) seek to inform and educate the public about the management problems it poses and to try to influence people coming to Snowdon to use the mountain in a way which will not accelerate its deterioration.'

With the aid of a £600 000 grant from the Countryside Commission, restoration work, including some resurfacing and drainage, has now taken place on all the footpaths and the summit area has been tidied up, with work on paved footpaths to the summit cairn also underway.

It has been apparent since the start of the management scheme that the first five years is only the initial phase, and that continuing care and management of Snowdon will require an ongoing commitment into the future.

Miners Path	68 000
Watkin Path	47 000
Pyg Track	44 000
Llanberis Path	32 000
Rhyd Ddu Path	19 000
Snowdon Ranger Path	17 000

4.16 Mount Snowdon: approximate footpath use June 1979–June 1980 (see Fig. 4.16 for paths)

13. In what ways do highland glaciated landscapes cater for the needs of those who enjoy active outdoor recreation?

14. Why are no further outdoor centres to be allowed in Snowdonia?

15. Explain how over-use has acted to the detriment of mountains such as Snowdon.

16. Describe the efforts made to stop the further deterioration of the mountain.

5

Rivers in the landscape

The physical landscape of rivers

Although glaciated landscapes such as those of the English Lake District, Snowdonia and the Scottish Highlands provide perhaps the most impressive scenery in the British Isles, the most important agent of erosion at work in shaping the landscape around us today is running water. As pebbles and stones are bounced along a river bed, we are reminded of the dynamic nature of the landscape around us. Although the rivers of Britain are generally quite short, in the course of their journeys from source to sea they change their character and that of the landscape through which they flow. Each river forms a system with its tributaries and occupies a basin which is made up of its catchment area surrounded by a watershed. As rivers flow along they ERODE material from their bed and banks, TRANSPORTING it to lower levels, finally DEPOSITING it on either their own valley floors or on the sea bottom.

In its upper course (Fig. 5.1) a river is engaged mainly in the process of EROSION or the gradual wearing down of its bedrock. The stream cuts downwards partly by dissolving the rock over which it flows — CORROSION, but more effectively by rolling or bouncing material such as stones and pebbles along its bed — CORRASION. Eddies of water swirl this material around on the river bed which is ground away to create potholes.

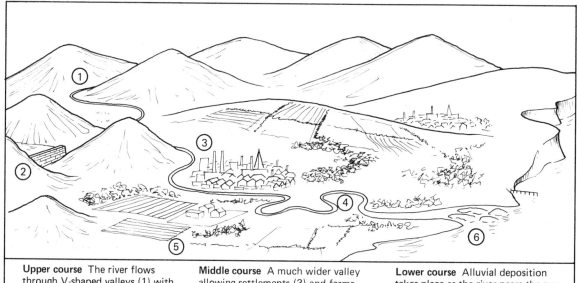

Upper course The river flows through V-shaped valleys (1) with interlocking spurs, *eroding* all the time. Some valleys (2) may be dammed to form reservoirs for water supply or hydro-electricity. These are often attractive tourist sites.

Middle course A much wider valley allowing settlements (3) and farms. Meanders (4) may be in evidence and the flood plain is often very intensively used. (5)

Lower course Alluvial deposition takes place as the river nears the sea. Deltas (6) may form if deposition is not removed by tidal scour. Such areas are of limited value as ports but recreation may be important.

5.1 A river landscape

These may eventually join up to lower the river bed into the underlying rock. The sides of the valley are also eroded — mainly by WEATHERING processes of wind, rain and frost action, and the result is the characteristic V-shaped valley with narrow floor and steep sides. These upper courses often make excellent sites for reservoirs (such as Kielder Water in the valley of the North Tyne in Northumberland), particularly where the site has a large water catchment area and an impermeable underlying rock.

Due to the geological diversity of the British Isles, as the river continues to cut deeper into its bed, it is likely to encounter rocks of varying hardness. Where the river flows over a band of hard, resistant rock, its profile is interrupted, and waterfalls or rapids may result. High Force in Upper Teesdale has been caused by the river crossing the Great Whin Sill, a hard layer of volcanic dolerite which is more resistant to erosion than the limestone bedrock further downstream. In other areas, rivers may flow around obstacles of resistant rock and, as a result, the course winds between interlocking spurs of higher ground.

In its middle course, the volume of water carried by the river increases as it is joined by more tributaries. The valley is much wider with a definite floor and the river may swing from side to side in a series of broad sweeps or MEANDERS which can be seen along the course of many British rivers, the Forth at Stirling, the Wear at Durham and the Severn at Shrewsbury are some of the more pronounced examples. In some cases, the inside of the meanders were attractive defensive sites for early settlers.

The lower, or flood plain, course of the river is marked chiefly by the process of deposition. Although erosion and transportation still continue, they are much reduced and the floor of the valley is often covered with deposits of fertile river-borne deposits or ALLUVIUM laid down during periods of flooding, with the coarser, heavier material deposited closest to the river and finer deposits further away. The flood plain is likely to be the most intensively used part of the river's course with agriculture, industry and settlement all in evidence. Conflict may arise as a result because all three land-uses compete for water, extracting what they need and, more seriously, often causing serious pollution by disposing of waste products and raw sewage directly into the river. These use up valuable oxygen in the water, and, if pollution is not checked, lead to the death of most forms of plant and fish life.

As it nears the sea, the river's current may slacken and its transportation power decreases leading to deposition. The presence of either an ESTUARY, or a DELTA tract at the mouth, is dependent upon the balance struck between the rate of river deposition and the rate at which the deposited material is removed by the sea. Where tidal scour, as this process is called, and long-shore sea-currents are sufficiently powerful, an estuary will result. Where the process of deposition is dominant, the river may reach the sea only by means of series of small channels called DISTRIBUTARIES winding between a maze of islands and sand shoals of deposition which together form a delta. The use of river mouths is clearly dependent on the degree to which people can control the rate at which deposition takes place. Wide, estuarine sites where deposition is limited, such as Milford Haven in Wales and Plymouth Sound, make excellent sites for port and harbour developments, but where sand bars, spits or deltas obstruct the mouth of the river, use by shipping is likely to be restricted to only small craft.

1. Draw out a table like the one below, using a whole page of your workbook, and complete the necessary details. Where possible, use examples from your local area.

	A River Landscape	
	Physical features	Use
Upper course		
Middle course		
Lower course		

2. Although river flood plains are usually fertile, they are seldom used for arable farming. Why not?

3. Why were many of Britain's early settlements such as Durham built on river meanders?

4. Explain why it is that some rivers have DELTAS at their mouths, whilst others have ESTUARIES.

5. Using your atlas, try to give three examples of each type of river mouth from:
   (i) British Isles
   (ii) Elsewhere.

Rivers and people: A study of the River Tyne

As mentioned in the previous section, rivers are used essentially for two main purposes. Firstly, fresh water is extracted from rivers and reservoirs

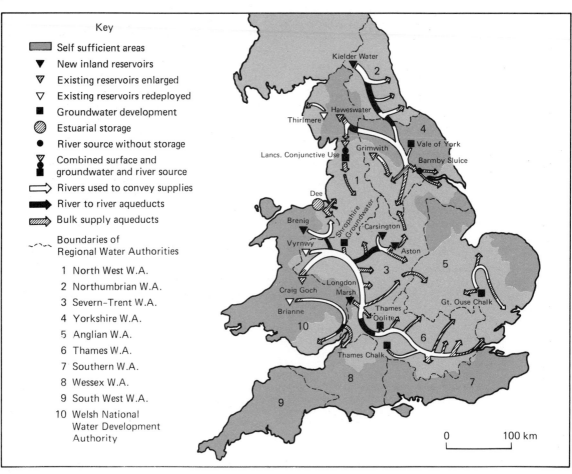

Key

- ▭ Self sufficient areas
- ▼ New inland reservoirs
- ▽ Existing reservoirs enlarged
- ▽ Existing reservoirs redeployed
- ■ Groundwater development
- ◍ Estuarial storage
- ● River source without storage
- ▮ Combined surface and groundwater and river source
- ⇨ Rivers used to convey supplies
- ⬛➤ River to river aqueducts
- ⬛⬛➤ Bulk supply aqueducts
- ⌇ Boundaries of Regional Water Authorities

1 North West W.A.
2 Northumbrian W.A.
3 Severn-Trent W.A.
4 Yorkshire W.A.
5 Anglian W.A.
6 Thames W.A.
7 Southern W.A.
8 Wessex W.A.
9 South West W.A.
10 Welsh National Water Development Authority

Map labels: Kielder Water, Haweswater, Thirlmere, Grimwith, Vale of York, Lancs. Conjunctive Use, Barmby Sluice, Dee, Brenig, Shropshire Groundwater, Carsington, Vyrnwy, Aston, Craig Goch, Longdon Marsh, Brianne, Thames Oolite, Gt. Ouse Chalk, Thames Chalk

0   100 km

5.2 The proposed National Water Grid for England and Wales

built along their course for domestic, agricultural and industrial purposes. Secondly, waste products and materials from these three sources are often dumped into rivers as an easy and cheap means of disposal. This case study of the River Tyne in north-east England looks at both of these aspects of a river's use, the problems caused, and the solutions which are being attempted.

Water supply

The severe drought which hit most of England in 1976 and 1984 revived the plans of the National Water Council to develop a National Water Grid for England and Wales (Fig. 5.2). The idea of transferring water from areas of surplus to areas of deficit is not new (Lake District to Greater Manchester, North Wales to West Midlands), but the suggestion of a combination of inland storage of water by reservoirs and groundwater with transfer possible to other parts of the country was a new idea. As the map shows, the concept of this 'National Grid' idea would be achieved by developing a network of rivers, aqueducts and tunnels to transfer water to different parts of the country. The development of a new reservoir in north Northumberland at Kielder Water on the River North Tyne forms an early step on the way towards this new water grid. Nevertheless the government made clear in 1984 that the cost of implementing the whole scheme made it unlikely that the stage shown in Fig. 5.2 will ever come to reality.

The Tyne is really three rivers. The River North Tyne rises on the Scottish border and flows in a south-easterly direction to join the River South Tyne, which rises in the North Pennines, near Hexham, to form the Tyne proper. In its upper reaches the river and its tributaries flow through bleak, unpopulated moorlands in steep, confined, V-shaped valleys, but it is the demands made upon it by the heavily populated areas in its lower course which have caused its present problems.

The Northumbrian Water Authority is responsible for an area of 930 000 hectares comprising the

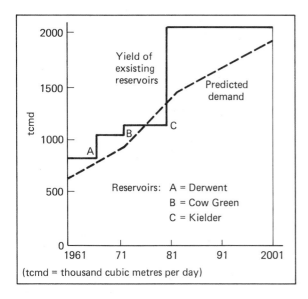

Yield of exsisting reservoirs

Predicted demand

Reservoirs: A = Derwent
B = Cow Green
C = Kielder

(tcmd = thousand cubic metres per day)

5.3 Water Supplies in Northumbrian Water Authority area

Metropolitan County of Tyne and Wear, Durham, Northumberland and Cleveland, as well as parts of North Yorkshire and Cumbria. The area served by the water authority is similar to Britain as a whole in that both have the heaviest rainfall in the north and west, and both have the greatest demand for water in the south and east. Fresh water requirements in the region rose from 630 thousand cubic metres per day (tcmd) in 1961, to 920 tcmd in 1971. Despite the industrial recession of the 1970s and early 1980s, the demand for water has continued to rise, although rather more slowly than originally predicted, and may reach 2000 tcmd by the year 2000. Although the water authority has been able to meet this extra demand by building new reservoirs at Derwent and Cow Green during the 1960s, water supply only just kept ahead of demand (Fig. 5.3) and a major new project — Kielder Water Reservoir was completed in 1982 to meet the demand for water in the region until well into the next century. Other possible schemes were investigated, but none

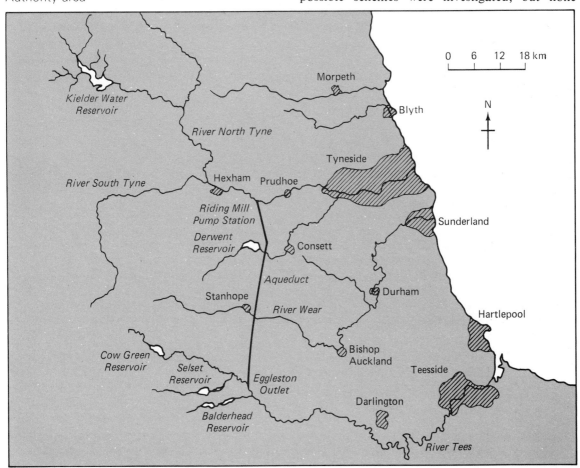

5.4 The Kielder Water Scheme

proved so suitable and any alternative would have involved constructing several smaller reservoirs to provide a yield comparable with that of Kielder Water.

The new reservoir has been built at the head of the North Tyne Valley between the villages of Kielder and Falstone. Covering 1086 hectares, it is the largest artificial lake in Europe with a storage capacity of 188 million cubic metres of water, it is larger than Ullswater and two-thirds the size of Windermere.

From the reservoir, water will flow down the course of North Tyne to Riding Mill (Fig. 5.4) a distance of 60 km. At Riding Mill some of the water will be transferred by pipeline and tunnel to the Rivers Wear (to Sunderland) and Tees (to Darlington and Middlesbrough). The rest of the water will continue to flow down the Tyne to Newcastle and the Tyneside conurbation. The scheme is therefore a major development in transferring water from areas of surplus (North Northumberland) to heavily populated, industrial regions such as Tyneside, Wearside and Teesside where demand is constantly increasing. One such major user of water is located next to the Tyne at Prudhoe, west of Newcastle where the huge Tissue Mill of Kimberly-Clark takes an average of 6500 cubic metres of water from the river each day. The

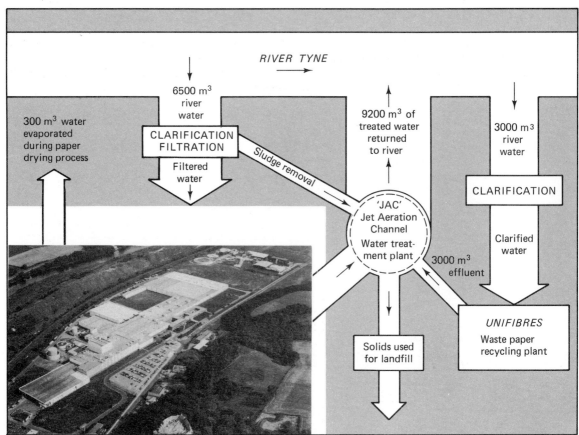

Kimberly-Clark Ltd., makers of the famous 'Kleenex' Tissue products opened this new Mill along the banks of the River Tyne at Prudhoe, in its middle course, in 1971. Large quantities of clean water are vital for this type of industry and as shown above, in 1982 the company took an average 6500m³ of water from the Tyne each day for the Paper Mill. The water is treated and filtered before being used. About 300m³ are lost to the atmosphere due to paper drying and the remaining 6200m³ each day is sent by pipeline to the company's Unifibres waste-paper recycling plant situated next to the Tissue Mill. Here the effluent is treated, along with that produced by the recycling plant itself, in a modern biological treatment plant (J.A.C.) where biological oxygen demand and solids are removed and treated water is then returned to the river.

5.5 Use of water by Kimberly-Clark Paper Mill at Prudhoe, Northumberland (figures shown are for average daily operations)

operation of the Mill, and its use of water is shown in Fig. 5.5.

Kielder Water (Fig. 5.6) is a very large artificial lake in Britain's biggest man-made forest. Although the potential of the North Tyne Valley for recreation was recognised as long ago as 1955 with the designation of the Borders Forest Park, the introduction of the new reservoir into the landscape has tremendously increased the recreational possibilities of the area. In the past, visitors were attracted to the area by the open moorlands and the facilities provided by the Forestry Commission. The construction of the reservoir has drowned a large section of the valley floor of the North Tyne, previously farmland, but has created instead a large body of open water with great potential for development as a recreation centre. The amenity value of the new lake is increased by its size and unusual shape with several small bays making ideal sites for both active and passive water sports. In the past visitors were limited due to the relative inaccessibility of the valley but some of the access roads have been improved for the heavy traffic involved in the construction work and the C200 road was realigned since its original course was drowned by the reservoir. The new demands for tourism have had to be reconciled with existing farming and forestry users. View points over the lake, picnic sites, camping areas, walking routes and car parks were all constructed in accordance with an overall master plan (Fig. 5.7) which was the result of cooperation between the Forestry Commission, which is responsible for land-based recreation activities, and the water authority which is responsible for Kielder Water itself.

Initial tests were carried out to decide whether motor boats should be allowed on the lake and it has been decided to permit their use, although speed boats and water-skiing are separate issues to be decided upon later; some concern has already been expressed about possible bank erosion which might result from these activities caused by wave creation. Swimming, sailing and canoeing are all regarded as acceptable activities and fishing has also been developed on the reservoir. Some of these sports have already had local competitions which attract many spectators as shown in photograph (Fig. 5.8) taken from the south shore showing sailing taking place on the lake. The

5.6 Kielder Water

master plan for recreation shows that these activities, and the associated car parks, picnic sites, toilets and information services are concentrated along the C200 road on the south side of the reservoir. Access to the north shore is not restricted, but can only be gained by ferry, on foot or on horseback in a deliberate attempt by the planners to 'zone' recreation so that a 'wilderness area' is retained around the north shore.

The scheme is a major development in both water supply and recreation provision and has already clearly established itself as a major tourist centre with more that half a million visitors in 1982, making it one of England's top 50 tourist attractions.

Apart from water supply and recreation, Kielder Water has also brought other advantages. A hydro-electric plant has been built into the dam and is linked directly to the National Electricity Grid at Spadeadam in Cumbria. Power will be generated 24 hours a day and the plant is able to produce enough electricity to supply a population of 12 000. Additionally, by controlling the volume of the water in the North Tyne, the scheme now provides a degree of flood protection for the valley. Undoubtedly however, the main benefit of the scheme lies in providing a reliable long-term water supply. The north-east of England is an area of high unemployment and an adequate water supply is a significant element in providing a regional infrastructure to attract new industries to the area and encourage the expansion of those already operating in the region.

6. What is meant by a NATIONAL WATER GRID? Outline the advantages which such a scheme would have in England and Wales.

7. By no means everyone has welcomed the idea of the Water Grid. Peter Simple, writing in the 'Daily Telegraph',—

"More reservoirs may be built, but the important contribution must come from the rivers which should no longer be treated as drains and sewers, but as regional water mains, carrying large volumes of water for long distances. Dammed and embanked, these once enchanted streams now face the worst of all. They are to become a system of water mains, inter-connected and turned on and off as water may be needed in this place or that in the giant conurbation that is England.

Who will any longer care, in the world of

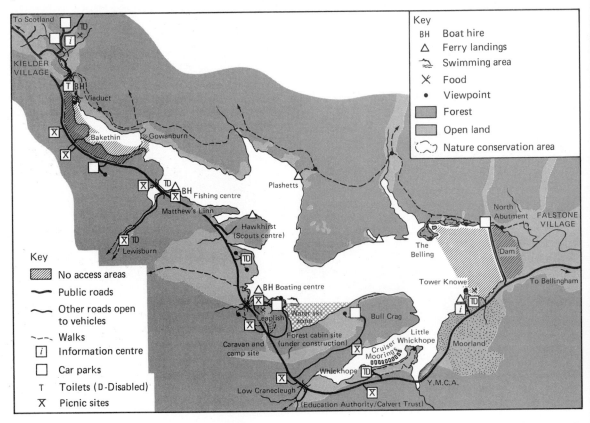

5.7 Recreational facilities at Kielder Water

5.8

environmental water engineers, if the river whose banks he stands on was once the Dove or the Avon? Who will be surprised if he sees the river dry up before his eyes, its water diverted by pressing a switch, to meet the demand for a thousand extra baths in Manchester or to help manufacture a thousand extra plastic ashtrays in Stevenage New Town?''
Do you agree with this view? Outline a possible reply to it.

8. Kielder Water was opposed at the planning enquiry. By whom, do you suppose, and for what reasons?

9. Describe the planned provision of recreation facilities at Kielder Water, and explain the differences planned between uses of the north and south shores of the lake.

Cleaning up the river

As well as being used as a source of fresh water to supply industrial and domestic users in its area, the River Tyne has also been used as an easy means of waste disposal — sewage and industrial effluent in particular, and this problem occurred mainly along the lower course of the river which is heavily populated (Fig. 5.4).

There were settlements at Newcastle and Gateshead in Roman Times and the riverside communities grew as trade began to develop — firstly coalmining, and then shipbuilding and engineering. Ninetenth century industrialists didn't really consider the environment too much — to have done so would have reduced their profits. As a result, huge amounts of industrial waste were discharged into the river and the sea, untreated, and practically unchecked. The deterioration of the river, and the low oxygen content of water resulted in the disappearance of migratory fish such as salmon and sea trout. The beaches near the mouth of the river, very popular with the urban population of Tyneside, were also affected.

When in flood, the river Tyne carries more freshwater out to sea than any other river in Britain, and local people were prepared to put up with smells which pervaded the area during hot, dry weather, in the knowledge that eventually the surface pollutants, concentrated in the upper layers of water, would flush out to sea. The situation was particularly acute during the 1976 drought, which reduced the freshwater flow in the river from a normal 4430 tcmd to about 318 tcmd, which was complemented by a similar volume of raw sewage. During that summer the smell from the river was noticeable 500 metres away on either bank. For decades, the Tyne had been described as an open sewer: the summer of '76 underlined that fact in the noses of a million Tynesiders! As early as 1936, Newcastle's Medical Officer of Health had noted in a report that practically every person who was immersed involuntarily in the River Tyne and survived drowning, contracted septic bronco-pnuemonia instead from the filth the river carried.

Although the problem of pollution was therefore officially recognised at an early date, a basic setback to controlling the use of the river as a dumping ground for waste, as with most British rivers, was the multitude of local authorities bordering the river banks. Clearly, one of these acting alone could not solve the problem, and along the Tyne there were no less than twenty separate such authorities, virtually all of which used the river for discharge of waste. In 1958 the Tyneside Joint Sewerage Board was created, and after ten years of argument, the proposed solutions to the problems were presented to the government in 1968.

The basic plan was a very simple idea, but very effective none the less. Previously all sewage was discharged into the river by outfalls running down the often steep banks and joining the river at right angles. The £110 million Tyneside Sewerage Scheme (Fig. 5.9) involves 73 km of new trunk sewers running parallel with the river banks to link up all 180 existing outfalls. They channel up to

1400 tcmd of sewage to the treatment works at Howdon on the north bank of the river (Fig. 5.10). Here the sewage flow is screened, grit is removed, sedimented and the treated liquid discharged into the river, minus about 70% of the waste. As well as treating large volumes of sewage formerly deposited straight into the river, the Howdon centre also directs the water flow from Kielder Water down the North Tyne and all parts of the Tyne water grid system. Sewage collected along the south bank sewer goes to a preliminary treatment works at Jarrow and from here it is transferred to Howdon by a syphon running underneath the river bed. The effluent from Howdon should be carried out of the river in the space of time taken by two tides. Hopefully, the scheme will allow the Tyne to complete the process of changing from a Department of Environment Class 4 River (grossly polluted) into a Class 1 (unpolluted). The early success of the scheme was reported in 1982 when checks revealed that pollution levels had fallen dramatically and fish had returned to the middle reaches of the estuary.

10. Explain why pollution in the Tyne was difficult to control.

11. Outline the main causes of the pollution and explain how the new sewerage scheme has attempted to deal with the problems you have identified.

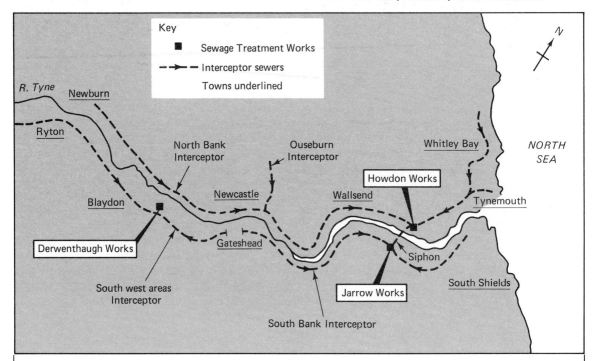

The £110 million scheme involved construction of 73 km of trunk sewers running parallel with the river and connecting 180 separate outfalls to a new treatment plant at Howdon on the north bank. Sewage from the south side of the river is sent first to a preliminary treatment plant at Jarrow and then by the Tyne syphon underneath the river to Howdon. After primary treatment at Howdon, the effluent will be returned to the estuary and the settled sludge shipped out to sea for deposition. Due to the high ridge of land which runs through Gateshead, the south-west of the region is served by a separate interceptor sewer to a new works at Derwenthaugh where the sewage from western Gateshead, Blaydon and Ryton areas will be collected and transferred by pipeline in a bridge over the river to link up with the system on the north bank until growth of demands makes it economic to build a local treatment plant. The scheme was officially opened by the Duke of Edinburgh in November 1981.

5.9 Tyneside joint sewerage scheme

5.10 The new Tyne Sewage Treatment Works at Howdon

6
Coastal Landscapes

In Chapter 1, we saw how the underlying rock types have been responsible for producing the great variety of landscapes found in the British Isles. Around the 5000 km of our coasts, in just the same way, the features which have been created are the result of the continual battle between the sea and the shoreline geology, which have together produced a coastline which is immensely varied. Fig. 6.1 shows a simplified classification of coastline changes which can be found in the British Isles. Generally, no part of the coast can be regarded as stable, rather the interaction between rock types and the sea has created dynamic landscapes which can be either ADVANCING, or being built up as a result of deposition, or else RETREATING, as a result of erosion.

In places, the sea is cutting back the cliffs and wearing away coastal rocks with dramatic results. The Holderness coast of Yorkshire, for example, suffers the worst coastal erosion in Europe and is thought to lie presently over 400 metres back from its position 200 years ago. This stretch of coast, between Bridlington and Spurn Head (Fig. 6.2), consists of soft boulder clay which has receded rapidly inland as a result of cliff collapse due to marine erosion at the base, combined with the constant weathering of the cliff face. The area is particularly prone to erosion when the North Sea

6.2 Part of the coast between Bridlington and Spurn Head

ADVANCING COAST

Deposition

Sand dunes
Spits
Bars and lagoons

Stable coastline

Stable coastline

Cliffs, arches
Stacks
Wave cut platforms

Erosion

RETREATING COAST

6.1 The dynamic coastline

is running high during severe winter storms and numerous villages along this coast which were recorded in the Domesday Survey of 1086 have disappeared beneath the sea and remain only as names on old maps and in historical records. Even where geology presents much more resistant rocks than boulder clay to the sea's onslaught, continual pounding by waves may create distinctive features around our coasts such as caves, arches, stacks and wave-cut platforms as the rocks are gradually eroded.

Where erosion does take place there is often very little that can be done. Sea-walls may cost up to £1 million for every kilometre and may then only last for thirty or forty years. Where sand and shingle are eroded and moved along a coast by longshore drift, the most common method of prevention used in Britain is the construction of groynes, or wooden structures built at right angles to the beach, but even these can cost up to £50 000 each if they are to be effective. In some places where groynes have been built, such as near Clacton in Essex, protection of one area of coast has only been achieved at the expense of another. By preventing long-shore drift, some parts of the coast are starved of material for their beaches, lose their best defence against the action of the sea as a result, and are then subjected to even greater erosion. Imaginative techniques have been used in various parts of Britain to retain or recreate beaches, particularly in resort areas where these are a vital part of the attraction to visitors. 'Beach-feeding', involving either dumping sand on the beach, or pumping it from off-shore has been tried at several British resorts, including Bournemouth and Portobello, near Edinburgh.

The second major feature of retreating coasts is caused by SUBMERGENCE, either due to a rise in sea-level or a fall in land level and as a result, an indented coastline is created with inlets or RIAS occupying the former coastal river valleys. It is estimated that the sea level around the British Isles rose by over 30 metres when the ice-sheets melted at the end of the last ice-age. Milford Haven in Wales, and the Fal estuary and Plymouth Sound in south-west England are all examples of this type of coastal feature, where submergence has affected an area in which river valleys, meeting the coast at right angles have been invaded by the sea.

In some parts of the British Isles, the rise in sea-level which was responsible for creating the rias, has been exceeded by an uplift of the land surface which has created the EMERGENT coastlines of Western Scotland. Here, the sheets of ice which covered most of the country, were very thick and their weight depressed the earth's crust. When average temperatures increased at the end of the ice age, this ice melted and ISOSTATIC UPLIFT of the land surface began, as these parts of the country gradually rose again.

The principal coastal features which have resulted from this emergence are the raised beaches found along the rugged west coast of Scotland, where they are often the only areas of flat land available for arable farming by the isolated crofting settlements.

The north-west coast of Scotland is also characterised by long, narrow inlets which have been occupied by the sea in post-glacial times. Unlike the ria coasts of south-west England and Wales, these fiords are the result of glaciation, and are not, in the Scottish case, due to submergence of the coast. As previously mentioned, the north-west coast of Scotland has actually risen considerably since the last ice-age. The Scottish fiords have been created because they were glacially overdeepened to such an extent that their floors and valley entrances were below sea level, and have remained so, despite the uplift which has taken place. When the sea-level rose, these glaciated coastal valleys were occupied by the post-glacial sea. These fiords offer few opportunities for settlement, but are amongst Scotland's most attractive coastal scenery and many have been designated as National Scenic Areas (Fig. 6.3).

In contrast to those areas of the coast previously mentioned which are being eroded by the action of the sea, in sheltered parts of the British Isles, muds, shingles and sands brought in and deposited have made it possible to reclaim land which was formerly occupied by the sea and these may even be used as valuable farmland. In Norfolk for example, it is estimated that over 3250 hectares have been gained from the sea since Roman times, and almost 15 000 hectares of the South Holland area of Lincolnshire have been reclaimed. More recently, deliberate planting of special marsh grasses such as *spartina townsendii*, which is capable of binding and holding silts and muds and preventing further erosion, has contributed to land reclamation around our coasts.

Unfortunately, where deposition takes place across river mouths creating spits, bars and lagoons, as in north-east Norfolk and Suffolk, the coastline consists of long stretches of shingle banks across river mouths which has prevented their use for navigation. Deposition of this type and shifting sandbanks around river mouths near

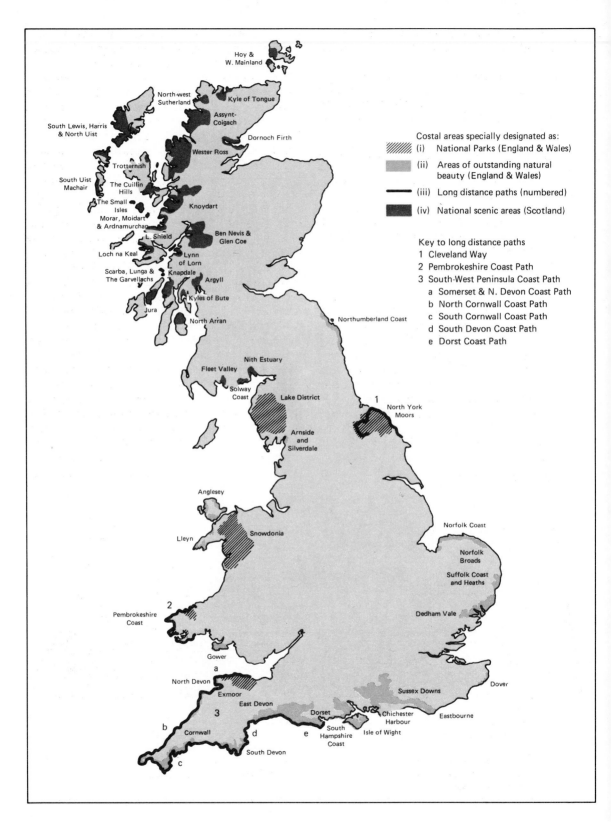

6.3 Coastal scenery in Britain

The labels and key on the map read:

Hoy & W. Mainland
North-west Sutherland
Kyle of Tongue
Assynt-Coigach
South Lewis, Harris & North Uist
Dornoch Firth
Wester Ross
Trotternish
South Uist Machair
The Cuillin Hills
The Small Isles
Knoydart
Morar, Moidart & Ardnamurchan
L. Shield
Ben Nevis & Glen Coe
Loch na Keal
Lynn of Lorn
Scarba, Lunga & The Garvellachs
Knapdale
Argyll
Kyles of Bute
Jura
North Arran
Northumberland Coast

Nith Estuary
Fleet Valley
Solway Coast
Lake District
North York Moors
Arnside and Silverdale

Anglesey
Lleyn
Snowdonia
Norfolk Coast
Norfolk Broads
Suffolk Coast and Heaths
Dedham Vale

Pembrokeshire Coast
Gower
North Devon
Exmoor
East Devon
Cornwall
South Devon
Dorset
South Hampshire Coast
Isle of Wight
Chichester Harbour
Sussex Downs
Eastbourne
Dover

Costal areas specially designated as:
(i) National Parks (England & Wales)
(ii) Areas of outstanding natural beauty (England & Wales)
(iii) Long distance paths (numbered)
(iv) National scenic areas (Scotland)

Key to long distance paths
1 Cleveland Way
2 Pembrokeshire Coast Path
3 South-West Peninsula Coast Path
  a Somerset & N. Devon Coast Path
  b North Cornwall Coast Path
  c South Cornwall Coast Path
  d South Devon Coast Path
  e Dorst Coast Path

some ports may mean that expensive dredging is necessary and the size of vessels has to be limited.

1. Outline some of the ways in which people have attempted to reduce the effects of coastal erosion in Britain and assess how far these efforts have been successful. You should refer to specific examples in your answer.

2. In some parts of the world, fiords are the result of submergence i.e. sea level has risen relative to the land. Explain how fiords in Scotland are different in origin.

3. With reference to specific examples from the British Isles, outline the main features and the main uses of:
   (a) Raised beaches;
   (b) Rias.

Coasts and people

The length and scenic variety of the British coastline, together with the fact that nowhere in the country is much more than 100 km from the coast, explains the popularity of coastal locations for many land-uses. Of these perhaps tourism is the most obvious and a vast industry has become based on Britain's many kilometres of sandy beaches with the more accessible locations developing as holiday resorts during the last century. Despite the unpredictability of the British climate, and the greatly increased popularity of foreign holidays, increased personal mobility and leisure time have together resulted in an increased use of coastal areas throughout the country.

An important historical factor in encouraging recreational use of the British coastline has been the common right of access to the foreshore which is owned mainly by the Crown. For centuries it has been illegal to fence in, or build on the foreshore which makes the narrow strip of coastal land around the British Isles by far the most important amenity in the country. Nevertheless, pressures on the coast come from many land-uses. Certainly, tourism continues to dominate in many areas, for example although Dartmoor in Devon is a popular National Park, (see Chapter 2), statistics indicate that of visitors to the county, only 5% make their way to Dartmoor compared with 85% who spend at least some of their time on the coast. A recent report has estimated that due to increasing pressures on the coastline, only about one-third can really be classed as 'unspoilt', and indeed in those parts of the country where coastal industry and urban development are most concentrated, the situation is much worse: in Kent over 50% and in Sussex over 70% of the coastline is built-up.

In an attempt to conserve the landscape and retain the areas of coast which are considered to be most attractive, various areas have been designated by the Countryside Commissions, (Chapter 7). As shown on Fig. 6.3, parts of the

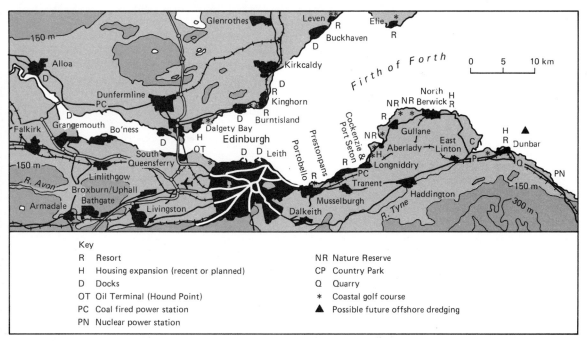

Key

R	Resort	NR	Nature Reserve
H	Housing expansion (recent or planned)	CP	Country Park
D	Docks	Q	Quarry
OT	Oil Terminal (Hound Point)	*	Coastal golf course
PC	Coal fired power station	▲	Possible future offshore dredging
PN	Nuclear power station		

6.4 The Forth Estuary — conflicting pressures on the coast coastline of England and Wales are now Areas of Outstanding Natural Beauty and some areas fall within the boundaries of the National Parks. In Scotland, much of the coast has been designated as National Scenic Areas. Developments within these areas are carefully monitored and those which might result in landscape deterioration, or increased pressure on resources, are often discouraged. Nonetheless, attempts have been made to make some of these areas more accessible to the population, particularly to those who are prepared to make some effort to get out and enjoy the scenery — hence the development of several long distance coastal footpaths which are also shown on Fig. 6.3.

Conflict over coastal land-uses is perhaps inevitable since, tourism apart, many kinds of industry favour coastal locations. Several estuarine ports in Britain, such as Bristol and Glasgow, have seen a movement away from the old dock areas developed during the last century close to the city centre. Instead, new developments are being located on coastal sites further down the estuary. On the Clyde for example, dock areas upstream have become disused and filled in as the increasing size of modern bulk cargo ships needed deeper berthing facilities which were only available downstream. As a result a new container terminal was built at Greenock, and a new iron ore terminal at Hunterston on the Ayrshire coast. Although the old dock areas retain their warehousing and storage facilities, the new motorway network has made possible the move towards the coast with very little disruption to distribution. Other industries such as petrochemicals, oil refining and associated industries have also developed in coastal locations as before the development of North Sea oil reserves, the country was dependent on imports, and even today, much of the raw material is still moved around in coastal tankers although some is now being moved by pipeline.

Although few industries are able to use sea water as a raw material, some, like power stations, have coastal locations in order to make use of water for cooling purposes, and others have in the past used the sea as an easy and cheap means of disposing of effluent. Many of these different coastal land-uses can be seen around the Forth Estuary on the east coast of Scotland (Fig. 6.4.).

4. Using Fig. 6.4 identify the different land-uses around the Forth Estuary and discuss how these might cause conflict between the various users of the coastline.

5. What attempts are being made to protect those parts of our coastline which are scenically the most attractive?

Case study: The Pembrokeshire Coast

Landscape

Located in south-west Wales, the quality and variation of the scenery of the Pembrokeshire Coast was recognised in 1952 when the area was designated as a National Park. It is the smallest of the ten parks and is the only one which is wholly coastal (Fig. 6.5), with only the industrial and port areas of Milford Haven and Pembroke in the south, and Fishguard in the north, excluded.

The landscape is one of great contrast and it has been said of the coastline that,"probably nowhere else in the British Isles is there so much variety in such a small area." The magnificent cliff coastline (around which extends the 270 km long Pembrokeshire Coastal Path, established in 1970) seldom exceeds more than 100 metres in height, but the variety of scenery owes more to the shoreline geology. Mostly the rocks are soft sedimentaries (Fig. 6.6) which have been eroded by the wave action of the sea to create broad, wide expanses of sandy bays which are immensely popular with summer visitors. St.Brides Bay, shown on Fig. 6.5, has been cut by the sea leaving the rugged, older, and more resistant rocks to the north and south as the headlands of St David's and Marloes-Dale. This pattern of bays and headlands is repeated on a smaller scale all around the coast and can be seen on the maps. Those in the south, such as Tenby, have developed into popular holiday resorts where the coastline is south-facing and sheltered from the prevailing westerly winds.

Much of the underlying rock is carboniferous limestone which can be easily dissolved and eroded by the sea. This has given rise to spectacular coastal features including SOLUTION HOLLOWS, BLOW-HOLES, GEOS and complex cave systems. Where these have collapsed, or where headlands have been attacked by the sea, natural arches such as The Green Bridge of Wales (Fig. 6.7) and stacks such as those at Elegug have been created.

In contrast to the effects of erosion by the sea, Milford Haven owes its origins more correctly to river erosion. The valley system of the River Cleddau was excavated when the sea level was much lower than at present before the last ice-age. With the post-glacial ice-melt, some 15 000 years

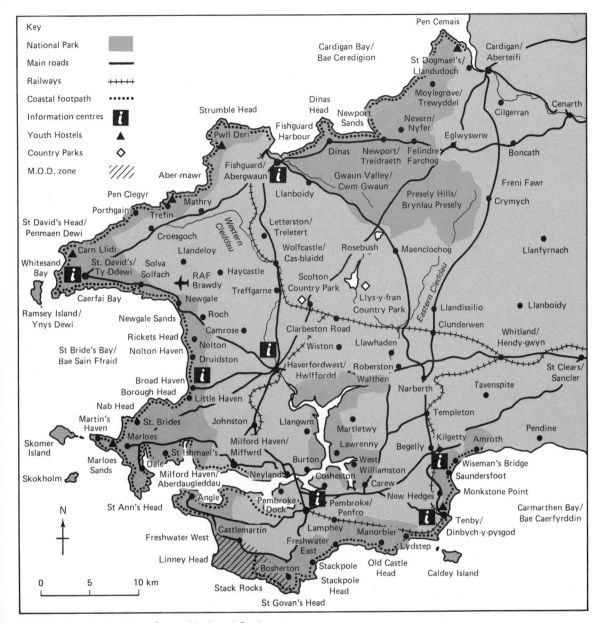

6.5 The Pembrokeshire Coast National Park

ago, huge volumes of meltwater were produced which flowed within the ice and in tunnels carved out beneath it. With the rise in sea-level the lower reaches of the Cleddau were effectively 'drowned' by the sea, creating the huge ria, of which Milford Haven is one of the best examples in Britain.

Tourism

The contrasting coastal scenery, together with one of the most mild climates to be experienced anywhere in Britain, have combined to make the Pembrokeshire Coast very popular with holiday-makers. The industry did not arrive with the designation of the National Park in 1952, in fact, resorts such as Tenby had flourished ever since the arrival of the railways during the nineteenth century which meant that the area was no longer so remote and inaccessible from the heavily populated areas of the south Wales coalfield to the east. Nevertheless, the main impetus of tourist-related developments has come within the last two decades with increased car ownership and leisure time. The result in Pembrokeshire has been change — to virtually every small village within

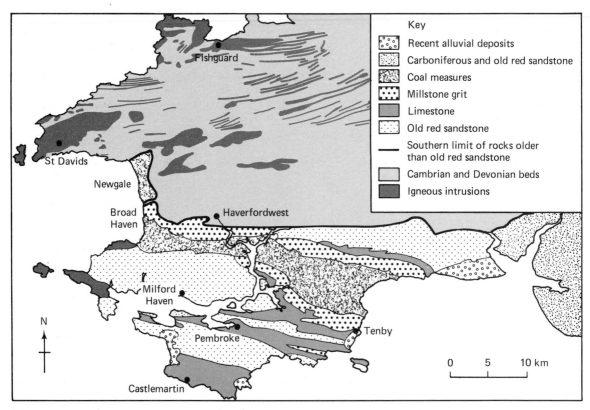

Key

- Recent alluvial deposits
- Carboniferous and old red sandstone
- Coal measures
- Millstone grit
- Limestone
- Old red sandstone
- —— Southern limit of rocks older than old red sandstone
- Cambrian and Devonian beds
- Igneous intrusions

6.6 South Pembrokeshire — outline geology

the National Park, particularly with the building of hotels, guest houses and caravan parks. The National Park Authority has had to attempt to reconcile the increasing requirements for more and larger beach car parks, wider roads to cope with higher volumes of traffic, more facilities for camping and caravan holidays, with the fundamental consideration of conserving the very landscape which has made the area so attractive to tourists in the first place. This problem has become even more acute within the last ten years or so with the growing trend away from hotel-based accommodation towards cheaper and more flexible camping, caravanning and self-catering holidays

The total income brought into the area each year from the tourist industry is second only to agriculture in the local economy, yet many farmers see tourism as a valuable additional source of income. Farms are small by the British average. Of 3466 holdings in the former county of Pembrokeshire, 1558 were less than 20 hectares in size, and only 83 over 100 hectares. Small size is usually coupled with lack of capital, inadequate buildings and small fields. Many smallholders are driven to supplement their income with bed and

6.7 The Green Bridge of Wales

breakfast visitors and all too often it is more profitable to grow "caravans rather than corn". The proliferation of small caravan sites has been discouraged by the National Park Authority, and instead farmers have been encouraged to take advantage of grants available to improve disused and often dilapidated farm buildings into holiday cottages and flats for tourists. Unfortunately, many farm cottages have been bought up by city dwellers as second homes, leaving over 50% of the houses in some coastal villages largely empty for much of the year. This has in some cases led to a decline of local communities as young people leave the area, unable to afford the inflated house prices which are a consequence of the 'second home phenomenon'.

Military and industrial use

Military use of land within the National Park boundary is a source of conflict. In the south, the Castlemartin tank ranges prevent public access to about 8 km of coast around Linney Head and denies the opportunity of seeing some of the finest carboniferous limestone cliff scenery in Britain. All the same, at least one observer has recently argued that although military use of land prevents public access, it often leaves wildlife surprisingly unaffected, and may even ensure relatively little damage occurs to the physical environment. Just to the north of Newgale, R.A.F. Brawdy is a main airforce test field, and many low-flying aircraft definitely disturb the peaceful villages of St David's and those along the broad coastal beach from Newgale to Broadhaven.

Milford Haven (Fig. 6.8) is without doubt one of the finest natural harbours in Europe. It is a long, sheltered ria, 2 km wide at its entrance and still over one kilometre in width at Pembroke Dock.(Fig. 6.9). In its lower reaches, the Haven is mostly deeper than 10 metres with a central channel of up to 20 metres in places. Since 1960 a major oil port has developed, second in Europe only to Rotterdam-Europort. Today three oil refineries operate around its shores with oil tankers making use of the deep water approaches and berths. Despite the size of these refineries, they have created less than 2000 local jobs and as Fig. 6.10 indicates, oil traffic using the port reached a peak in 1974, after which a combination of factors, including the massive rise in the price of Middle East oil, the development of North Sea oil reserves, and the industrial recession of the late 1970s and early 80s, have prevented a recovery in trade. This was reflected in the closure of the Esso refinery on the north shore in March 1983.

The decline in the use of Milford Haven has been particularly marked by the fall in the number of Very Large Crude Carriers or V.L.C.C.s. During the early 1970s, these huge ships, often over 250 000 tonnes were seen as a vital part of oil movements. The decline in imports and increased use of North Sea Oil, which can be shipped around our coasts in smaller vessels economically, saw a fall in the number of V.L.C.C.s using Milford Haven from over 200 in 1974 to 52 in 1982, with every indication that numbers will continue to decrease.

One of the problems caused by the presence of the oil refineries is that of visual landscape intrusion. Although mostly located outside the National Park boundary, and despite expensive landscaping attempts, the visual impact (Fig. 6.8) has been described by one local writer as being 'both widespread and corrosive'.

Clearly, the second major problem has been the

6.8 Milford Haven

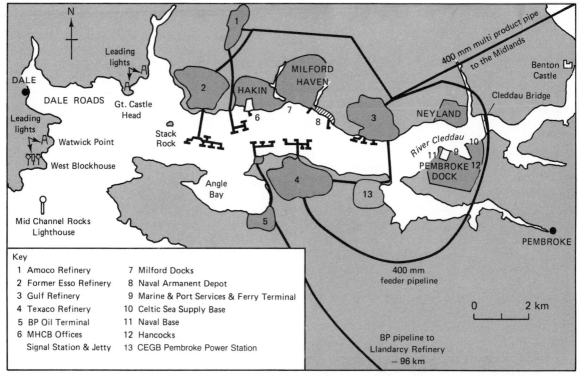

6.9 The port of Milford Haven

prevention of oil pollution within the Haven, the shores of which are mostly bordered by the National Park. The problem is constantly being monitored by the Milford Haven Conservancy Board and has been successfully overcome by a policy which insists on safe operational procedures both on the ships which use the Haven, and also at the terminals where they berth. During the earlier years as an oil-handling port, the number of pollutions which occurred annually peaked at 83 incidents, but this has gradually been reduced to an all-time low of 21 incidents in 1982, illustrating the effectiveness of the campaign of the Conservancy Board against oil pollution. Indeed, since some of the incidents recorded involved spills of less than 50 litres, pollution can be seen to be minimal, especially when viewed against the volume of oil handled at the port.

The availability of oil from the refineries encouraged the Central Electricity Generating

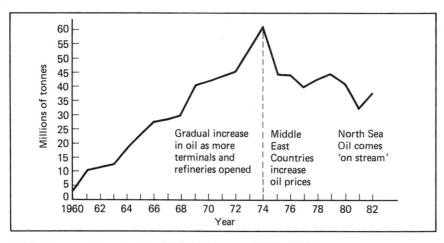

6.10 Oil cargo handled in Milford Haven, 1960–1982

Board to construct one of Europe's largest oil-fired power stations at Pembroke. Although the station is outside the National Park, its 213 metre high chimney pours out 650 tonnes of sulphur gases each day and cannot be regarded as one of the area's tourist attractions. Furthermore, the 400 Kv power grid lines and pylons carrying the electricity to the supergrid link at Swansea, Cardiff and Bristol, intrude aggressively on the Pembrokeshire landscape, despite being routed to avoid the National Park itself.

To compensate to some extent for the decline in the use of Milford Haven by oil traffic, a new use has been the development of commercial passenger traffic to Ireland. In 1970 the B. & I. line began a service to Cork from a new ferry terminal at Pembroke Dock and a further service, to Rosslare, was inaugurated in 1980. Unfortunately, largely due to the Irish economic recession, the Cork service was suspended late in 1982, but the Rosslare service continues to operate.

The most recent, and certainly most unusual change in the use of the port came in 1983, with the announcement that the Welsh Water Authority had taken over the storage facilities at the former Esso oil refinery to supply water to the Middle East! The idea came from new pollution-reducing regulations which favour the idea of fresh water being backhauled to the Middle East as ballasting for oil tankers. The water will be suitable for irrigation use without further treatment. The Authority's Llys-y Fran reservoir (Fig. 6.1) will be used to supply the water to the holding tanks at Milford Haven to support the loading rate of 227 000 cubic metres, or over 50 million gallons, each day. The success of the scheme is being promoted by the government and leaflets have been produced in English, French and Arabic to promote the project to possible customers, particularly in areas such as the Middle East, where water shortages are frequent.

Apart from industrial development, Milford Haven's potential for recreation is considerable. Over 1200 moorings provide facilities for sailing, motor boating, water-skiing, fishing and swimming. Plans are currently underway to investigate the possibility of developing a yachting marina. Clearly the changing use of this stretch of our coastline is continuing.

6. Describe how geology has influenced the landscape of the Pembrokeshire coast. Use Figs. 6.5 and 6.6 to help you and mention specific locations in your answer.

7. Outline the advantages and disadvantages which the tourist industry has brought to Pembrokeshire.

8. Compare and contrast the pressures on the Pembrokeshire coastline (Fig. 6.5) at:
   (a) Castlemartin;
   (b) Tenby;
   (c) Milford Haven.

9. Using Fig. 6.10, explain the changes in the volume of oil traffic using Milford Haven.

10. Describe and explain the changing nature of the use made of Milford Haven referring to oil, water exports, ferry traffic and recreation.

7

Landscape and nature conservation in the the countryside

Approximately 80% of Britain's population live within urban areas which have spread and encroached upon our countryside at an alarming rate during this century. With a population approaching 56 million, in a country which only extends to 24 million hectares, we are one of the most densely populated countries in the world: although this disguises considerable regional variations within the British Isles. Consequently, the pressures on countryside in this country are considerable, and various measures have been required in order to conserve something of what does remain for future generations. Few people would argue that these measures are now complete, but at least a start has been made.

The role of official agencies

1. The Countryside Commissions The official agency which is charged with responsibility for conserving the countryside is the Countryside Commission (in Scotland, the Countryside Commission for Scotland). These government-funded organisations were established as one of the far-reaching consequences of the 1968 Countryside Act. Basically, their powers and responsibilities are 'to conserve and enhance the natural beauty of the countryside and to encourage the provision and improvement of countryside facilities for open-air recreation by the public'. They also have a statutory duty to advise the government and local authorities on all aspects of countryside matters. One of the Countryside Commissions' ongoing duties is to recommend areas of natural beauty for 'DESIGNATION'. This power to designate can be applied in a variety of different ways and with varying degrees of effectiveness. The predecessor of the Countryside Commission in England and Wales, which was called the National Parks Commission, helped establish the ten NATIONAL PARKS (Fig. 7.1) during the 1950s,

under the 1949 National Parks and Access to the Countryside Act. Their designation during that decade helped to conserve the most important WILDERNESS areas in England and Wales, and they remain so to this day, largely as a result of that action. In Scotland, where areas of WILDSCAPE cover a much larger proportion of the country, and where urban pressures were not nearly so great in the late 1940s, no National Parks were actually established, but five NATIONAL PARK DIRECTION AREAS were identified in 1948 (Fig. 7.12). In these areas, government maintains planning oversight in order to retain their essential character. In addition, and very much more recently, some 40 NATIONAL SCENIC AREAS (Fig. 7.1) have also been designated, and there local planning authorities are obliged to consult the Countryside Commission for Scotland where certain specified classes of development are concerned.

The 1949 National Parks Act did not only legislate for the designation of national parks in England and Wales, it also sought to identify AREAS OF OUTSTANDING NATURAL BEAUTY (A.O.N.B) (Fig. 7.1). There are now 35 of these covering more than 9000 km ^{2}, and with the possibility of five or six more in the near future. In total, this ensures that about one-fifth of the countryside in England and Wales is protected by National Park or A.O.N.B. status. Other designations carried out by the Countryside Commission include HERITAGE COASTS and LONG DISTANCE FOOTPATHS (Fig. 7.1)

2. The Nature Conservancy Council The 'sister' organisation to the Countryside Commissions which operates within the realm of nature or wildlife conservation is the Nature Conservancy Council (N.C.C.) which replaced the Nature Conservancy in 1973. Also a government-funded organisation, its jurisdiction extends over all of Great Britain and its functions include:

a) the establishment and management of nature reserves;

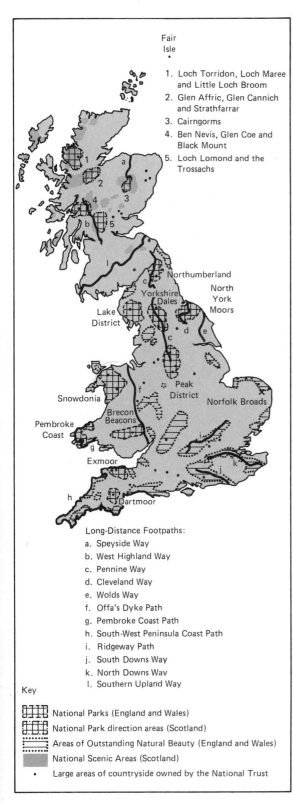

Fair Isle

1. Loch Torridon, Loch Maree and Little Loch Broom
2. Glen Affric, Glen Cannich and Strathfarrar
3. Cairngorms
4. Ben Nevis, Glen Coe and Black Mount
5. Loch Lomond and the Trossachs

Northumberland
Yorkshire Dales
North York Moors
Lake District
Snowdonia
Peak District
Norfolk Broads
Pembroke Coast
Brecon Beacons
Exmoor
Dartmoor

Long-Distance Footpaths:
a. Speyside Way
b. West Highland Way
c. Pennine Way
d. Cleveland Way
e. Wolds Way
f. Offa's Dyke Path
g. Pembroke Coast Path
h. South-West Peninsula Coast Path
i. Ridgeway Path
j. South Downs Way
k. North Downs Way
l. Southern Upland Way

Key

National Parks (England and Wales)

National Park direction areas (Scotland)

Areas of Outstanding Natural Beauty (England and Wales)

National Scenic Areas (Scotland)

· Large areas of countryside owned by the National Trust

7.1 Countryside conservation in Britain

b) the provision of advice to government, local authorities and the general public;
c) the commissioning and support of nature research.

Some 189 National Nature Reserves (Fig. 7.2) have now been created by the N.C.C. and these cover more than 142 200 hectares. Much of this land is not owned by the N.C.C. but is leased from private landowners, or has been subject to special agreements to ensure protection. Another of the tasks undertaken is the identification of Sites of Special Scientific Interest (S.S.S.I.) which are deemed to be such because of their flora, fauna, geological or physiographical features. The 1949 legislation under which these are identified does not allow for the ownership of S.S.S.I. by the N.C.C. but the Council can enter into agreements

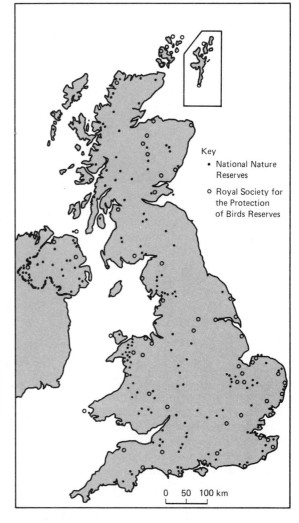

Key
· National Nature Reserves
○ Royal Society for the Protection of Birds Reserves

0 50 100 km

7.2 National Nature Reserves in Britain

to conserve them and must be consulted by local planning authorities over any development proposals relating to them. There are now 3356 S.S.S.I. throughout Great Britain.

3. The Forestry Commission Although the Countryside Commissions and the Nature Conservancy Council are the two official agencies charged with conservation as their major functions, various other bodies do have this as one of their lesser functions. Perhaps the most prominent of these is the Forestry Commission, who have as their principal objective:

'the efficient production of wood for industry, either existing or projected',

but who also have as one of their subsidiary objectives:

'to protect and enhance the environment'.

Being the major landowner in Britain, with forests throughout the country (Fig. 7.3) it is absolutely vital to our heritage that this objective is pursued to the full, and that good practice in sympathetic landscaping and planning of forests, and in wildlife conservation is encouraged. Many first generation forests, planted soon after the Commission was set up in 1919, were criticised as being, 'like green blankets thrown over the landscape', but as these forests have matured, the interests of visual amenity, as well as the economic harvesting of the trees, have been taken into account. The felling areas selected have deliberately been of a variety of sizes, shapes and locations so as to break up the geometrical outlines of the original forests. More recent forests have been designed to blend in more with the landscape, to lie below, rather than to dominate the skyline, and to follow the natural curves of the land. They have been planted with a variety of tree types to prevent one block of colour standing out, and often incorporate broadleaved and deciduous trees, especially along the forest fringes, in order to add interest and contrast to the edges of the woodland area.

Within the field of wildlife conservation, the Commission has identified two main aims:

'to safeguard its woodland and wildlife habitats, and where practicable, to improve them', and

'to give particular attention to these sites where nature conservation has been identified as of special importance'.

In practice, these aims are carried out in a variety of ways, for example, the margins of plantations are often left in a semi-natural state along with other 'fringe' areas beside paths, tracks, streams and ponds. Scrub woodland and broadleaved trees may be left as a sanctuary for wildlife, while the

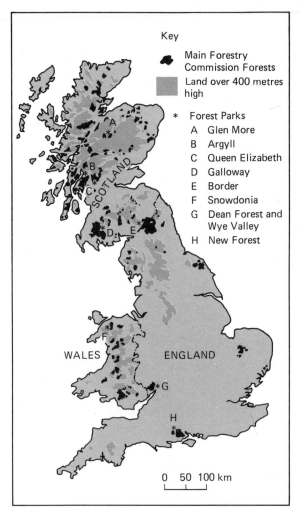

Key

⬤ Main Forestry Commission Forests

▨ Land over 400 metres high

✳ Forest Parks

A Glen More
B Argyll
C Queen Elizabeth
D Galloway
E Border
F Snowdonia
G Dean Forest and Wye Valley
H New Forest

0 50 100 km

7.3 The distribution of Forestry Commission woodlands

surrounding area is prepared and planted. Unnecessary 'tidying up' is often avoided as well. One animal which requires active management, in order to keep tree damage and loss to a minimum, is the deer, and annual culls are required in certain forests to maintain an appropriate deer population. Inevitably, there are occasions when the requirements to expand commercial forestry and the need for conservation do come into conflict. In Britain this is probably most true in uplands, particularly the high moorland areas, where the growth of coniferous forests must drastically change the existing landscape and irrevocably alter wildlife habitats.

1. Within which broad fields of conservation lie the responsibilities of:

a) The Countryside Commission;
b) The Nature Conservancy Council?

2. List what each of the above two bodies are empowered to designate.

3. Why is the power of designation so vital to these official agencies?

4. Describe the distribution of Forestry Commission woodland in Britain (Fig. 7.3) and explain why the Commission's role in conservation is so important within the context of this distribution.

5. Construct a table listing the measures open to the Forestry Commission to assist:
a) Landscape conservation
b) Nature Conservation
Add a suitable title to the table.

The role of local authorities

Even in the nineteenth century, urban-based people demonstrated a desire to 'conserve' certain areas of land within built-up areas and 'to bring the countryside into the city' by the creation of parks. These urban parks (Fig. 7.4) are cherished by many who live in cities. Although most of them have been consciously planned and laid out to include large areas of grass and water and lines of trees, they do provide much needed space and an interruption to the building pattern found in our cities. Most of these urban parks were established by local authorities whose responsibilities have been extended more recently by the Countryside Acts (1967 in Scotland, 1968 in England and Wales) which granted them the powers to create so-called 'Country Parks' (Fig. 8.1) in areas around the urban fringe. Certain of these Country Parks, which vary enormously in size and character have left 'wild' areas deliberately unplanned within their perimeters in order to provide for conservation to a limited extent.

The role of voluntary bodies

Apart from the offical agencies, voluntary bodies have been playing an increasingly important role in preserving the countryside and nature of Britain. Very often, these voluntary bodies have specialist interests which dictate that they seek to acquire or manage landscapes with particular qualities.

The National Trust is the voluntary body which has perhaps done most to safeguard Britain's scenic and cultural heritage for the nation. Its more well-known role is in preserving historic buildings, but it also owns large areas of countryside in some of the wildest and most natural remaining parts of the British Isles (Fig. 7.1). In the Lake District of England alone, 54 000 hectares of fell, lake and forest are protected. In Scotland, wild and beautiful areas such as Ben Lawers and Torridon, and islands such as St Kilda and Fair Isle come under National Trust for Scotland management. Similarly, in Northern Ireland, the western shoreline of Strangford Lough and, in Wales, parts of Snowdonia, the Cambrian Mountains and the Brecon Beacons are conserved by the National Trust.

In many ways preservation of wildlife in Britain has been a much greater focus of attention than preservation of countryside. This, in part, has been due to the efforts of the Nature Conservancy Council, but also to publicity conscious organisations such as the Royal Society for the Protection of Birds (R.S.P.B) and various wildlife trusts which have been highly successful in mobilising public support for their respective causes. The R.S.P.B. itself now has over 360 000 members and manages 93 reserves (some deliberately unannounced). They range from the small island seabird colonies of the Forth and Coquet to the extensive flats and salt-marshes of Morecambe Bay and Langstone Harbour and from the upland oakwoods of Gywnedd and Killiecrankie, to the lonely flood meadows of the Ouse Washes and West Sedgemoor (Fig. 7.2).

A park system for the U.K.?

The work done by these voluntary bodies in countryside and nature conservation in many ways complements and adds to the designated framework established by official agencies and local authorities. In Britain, the provision for conservation and a park 'system' have gradually evolved over time and a more coherent strategy of management is beginning to emerge. Although various parts of the conservation and parks 'system' jigsaw have been established at different times, in rather a piecemeal fashion, some sort of structure (Fig. 7.4) can now be identified.

In England and Wales, the lynchpin of the conservation aspect of this park 'system' has been and will remain, the National Parks. Each of these has its own cultural and landscape quality and characteristic flora and fauna which must continue to be rigorously conserved (Fig. 7.5). Unfortunately, it appears unlikely that further semi-natural landscapes will be conserved in this way in the near future, although overtures have

Type	Examples	When Established	Size	Planning	Provision
Urban Parks	LONDON: Hyde Park, Regents Park EDINBURGH: Princes St. Gdns	Since nineteenth century	Small	Formally planned out, often with ponds, grass areas, surfaced paths etc.	Mostly for fairly passive forms of recreation.
Country Parks (see Fig. 8.1)	ENGLAND: Sherwood Forest, Clumber SCOTLAND: Strathclyde, Culzean	Since 1967 in Scotland; 1968 in England and Wales	Still fairly small, but larger than Urban Parks	Partially planned out, perhaps with some retained wild areas.	Usually provision for both active and passive forms of recreation. Ranger services often available.
Forest Parks (see Fig. 7.3)	ENGLAND: Forest of Dean & Wye Valley SCOTLAND: Glen More WALES: Snowdonia N. IRELAND: Castlewellan	First one (Argyll) in 1935, others followed in late 30s, 40s, 50s	Vary	Perhaps with forest walks and nature trails, but left as 'natural' as possible.	Special provision for public access and recreation within restricted areas.
Nature Reserves, Wildlife Sanctuaries (See Fig. 7.2)	SCOTLAND: Beinn Eighe ENGLAND: Upper Teesdale	Since 1949 for N.N.R.'s	Vary	Normally left as natural as possible.	Observation facilities sometimes provided, but few others. Often a resident warden on site.
National Parks (Fig. 7.1)	ENGLAND: Exmoor Northumberland Peak District WALES: Brecon Pembrokeshire coast	Since 1949, during the 1950s	Very large	Existing land-uses conserved as far as possible.	Managed to satisfy twin aims of conservation and recreation. Attempts to maintain landscape quality and resist development. Tourism/recreation in specific zones.

7.4 A park system for the U.K.?

been made in the past about the Cambrian Mountains in Wales (eventually rejected in 1973), and more recently about the Norfolk Broads in East Anglia, where the Broads Authority was established in 1980. It is appropriate that the case study which follows is of a National Park with truly unique qualities of landscape, the conservation of which must be a priceless asset to the nation.

6. How has the role of local authorities been extended in recent years in relation to the provision of park recreation?

7. Study Fig. 7.1. Suggest why organisations such as The National Trusts have continued to add to their countryside properties even within the National Parks.

8. Why do organisations such as The National Trusts and the R.S.P.B. seek to acquire or manage land in such diverse areas?

9. List the original development of the different types of 'park' in chronological order (Fig. 7.4). What does this suggest about the way in which the U.K. parks 'system' has developed?

10. Attempt to classify the National Parks identified in Fig. 7.5 into different landscape types. Justify your classification.

Brecon Beacons (1344 km²): rising in Pen y Fan to nearly 900 metres. Largely sandstone moorland with some limestone, only interrupted by wooded gorges. Largely unthreatened by development; still a farming are with open moorland fringed by enclosed pasture. Although the nearest park to London, its scenery remains virutally unspoilt.	**North York Moors** (1432 km²): this park extends inland from some of the highest cliffs in eastern England, to the largest heather moors in any National Park. The Cleveland Hills, within the park, rise to 458 m at Urra Moor. Beautiful narrow valleys such as Farndale and Rosedale contribute to the splendour of the central part of the park. The most contentious development occurs around Whitby where potash is mined at Boulby. The Cleveland Way footpath runs through the park.
Dartmoor (945 km²): largest remaining area of elevated wilderness left in southen England. Much of Dartmoor remains open moor but its wild quality is accentuated by its mires and heather. Its periphery is incised with oakwood-filled gorges. Relics of ancient man abound and mark the continual occupance of the area by man for over 4000 years. Under threat from various developments , most of which were in existence before the park was designated in 1951. (See Chapter 2)	**Peak District** (1404 km²): this National Park forms the southernmost part of the Pennines and was Britain's first. Like the Lake District, it too has its own Special Planning Board which contributes to the Peak's 'well-run' reputation. Most of the park consists of millstone grit moorlands, notably the 'Dark Peak' in the north, but the 'White Peak' in the south is largely limestone dales. Fluorspar and limestone are extracted and detract most from scenery.
Exmoor (686 km²): a National Park of superb heather moorland and magnificent coastline lying mainly in Somerset, but partly within Devon. Farming landscapes within Exmoor have been subject to particular change with the heather moorland suffering rapid encroachment from reclamation and enclosure. At the same time, sheep farming has been replaced by more intensive agriculture.	**Pembrokeshire Coast** (583 km²): as the smallest of the ten National Parks, this one contains no mountains, just 272 km of dramatic coastal landscape including spectacular cliffs and wave-cut platforms. Within the National Park lies part of the fine deep water ria, Milford Haven, used as an oil terminal, although most of the refineries are excluded from the park, their visual impact is considerable. Other potential conflicts arise from military use, with the Castlemartin Tank Zone and RAF Brawdy. (See Chapter 6).
Lake District (2243 km²): the largest of the National Parks and one of the two which has its own planning authority. This area inspired the so-called 'Lakeland poets' to wax lyrical about its terrific variety of landscape within such a small area. Now under pressure from its millions of visitors each year. The 'waters' themselves, of which there are 17 in all, have been the subject of conflict in the past (See end of this chapter).	**Snowdonia** (2171 km²): the glaciated mountain splendour of this part of north-west Wales, is the heart of the Welsh language and culture. Contains 14 peaks above 900 metres in height, attracts mountaineers and hillwalkers from all areas and provides for many other outdoor pursuits. During this century large areas of conifers have been planted and various other of the areas resources are tapped for power production, water supply and roofing slate (See chapter 4).
Northumberland (1031 km²): the most northerly of the National Parks lying next to the border with Scotland and encompassing two hill ranges: the Cheviots and the Simonside Hills. The southern boundary of the park is marked by the Roman or Hadrian's Wall, Military training areas cover a large part of the northern area of the park and afforestation has continued apace this century, most notably in the Wark forest, to the south of the River North Tyne.	**Yorkshire Dales** (1761 km²): this is the landscape described by James Herriot in his 'vet' books. The park straddles the central Pennines including high moorlands, and the dales between with their drystone walls and stone houses. In the south, the limestone scars and pavements add variety to the scenery, but limestone quarrying has had an adverse effect on scenery. (See Chapter 3).

7.5 National Park 'pen protraits'

Case study: The Lake District National Park

The Lake District is the largest of the ten National Parks in England and Wales (Figs. 7.1, 7.5). Designated in 1951, this Park contains a variety of landscape perhaps unique in the British Isles. It is this unique variety of landscape, long recognised in the verse of such 'Lakeland poets' as Wordsworth and Coleridge, and by generations of tourists, which made it the obvious choice as one of the earliest National Parks.

This variety is in part due to the highly complex underlying structure of the Lake District with rock types of igneous, metamorphic and sedimentary origin (Fig. 7.6). Each of these rock types has contributed to its own highly characteristic scenery, from the craggy and rugged mountains

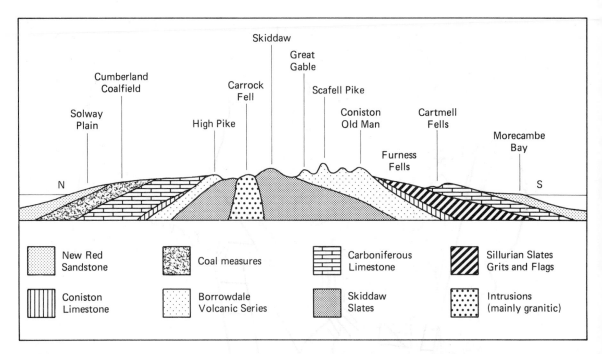

7.6 Cross-section N.S. across the Lake District

Legend:
- New Red Sandstone
- Coal measures
- Carboniferous Limestone
- Sillurian Slates Grits and Flags
- Coniston Limestone
- Borrowdale Volcanic Series
- Skiddaw Slates
- Intrusions (mainly granitic)

belonging to the Borrowdale Volcanic Series to the conical but smooth-sided mountains of Skiddaw Slates and the lower plateau and valley country associated with the Silurian Slates (Fig. 7.7). Since its formation, the dome-shaped structure (Fig. 7.6) of the Lake District has been subjected to repeated glaciation which has caused the removal of the original surface rocks and the development of its superimposed radial drainage pattern. The remnants of this past glacial and fluvial action remain today and further contribute to the great variety of landforms in the Lake District.

The vegetation, which forms another piece in the landscape jigsaw of the Lake District, has also undergone change through time, the major influences perhaps being: the gradual disappearance of native woodland, the development of sheep farming during the nineteenth century, and the establishment of extensive areas of commercial coniferous forest during this century. However, all points remembered, the visitor's lasting memory of the Lake District landscape is likely to be of an area of great scenic beauty, with imposing mountains, open fells and deep glaciated valleys, floored by long ribbon lakes.

Prior to the designation of the area as a National Park, the Lake District had been suffering increasing pressure from a variety of types of development which threatened its unique environment in various ways. One of the most important duties of the Lake District Special Planning Board, the body created as the sole planning authority within the National Park, has been to reconcile the often conflicting needs of conservation and development, and to resolve the particular land-use conflicts which have occurred (Fig. 7.8). In this task, the Board has had the co-operation of the other major agencies which own

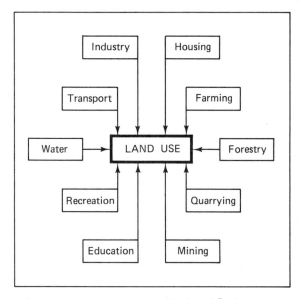

7.8 Conflicting interests in National Parks

7.7 View of Keswick and Derwentwater from Skiddaw

land in the Park (Fig. 7.9) as well as private landowners.

One particularly contentious issue which has regularly given rise to conflict has been the piping of water from several of the lakes for use in towns around the periphery of the Lake District, and, even more controversial, its 'export' to the Greater Manchester conurbation. At present, as can be seen from Fig. 7.10, the water resources of the western Lake District are 'tapped' by several of the industrial towns of West Cumbria, and those of the eastern Lake District for use in and around Manchester. Several schemes to extend water extraction are at present under consideration. For example, the proposals by British Nuclear Fuels Ltd. (B.N.F.L.) and the North West Water Authority, to draw more water from Ennerdale Water and Wastwater to supply

the B.N.F.L. plant at Sellafield on the Cumbrian coast, and domestic users in west Cumbria.

In other areas, however, attempts to reconcile the demands from competing forms of land-use have been considerably more successful. The Forestry Commission is one organisation which has had some success in 'marrying' the needs of forestry, amenity, conservation and recreation in various of the small forests within the National Park, but perhaps most notably in Grizedale Forest (Fig. 7.11). There, near Coniston Water, facilities include: car parking, a camp site, nature trails, forest walks, a wildlife centre and deer museum (Fig. 7.13). Some of the greatest development pressures have resulted from increasing numbers of people who visit the Park each year (12 million in recent years) because of increased leisure time, greater accessibility as a

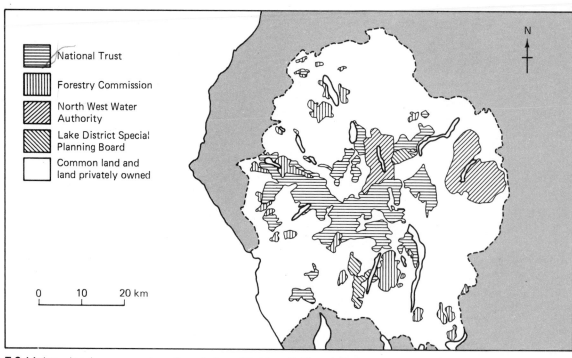

7.9 Major land-owners in the Lake District National Park

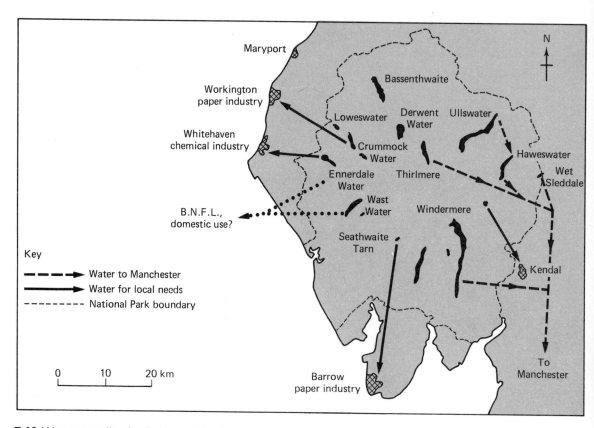

7.10 Water supplies in the Lake District

1. Development:	Formed 1937 when Forestry Commission bought Grizedale Hall Estate. Consists today of 3515 hectares of which:
	
	        coniferous woods: 2650 ha.
	        broadleaved woods: 357 ha.
	        farmland: 285 ha.
	        other land: 179 ha.
	        housing: 44 ha.

2. **Geology Climate:**	Underlying rock is mainly shales with volcanic intrusions. Soils are degraded and eroded with extensive areas of peat on higher ground. Rainfall decreases eastwards with average of 1800 mm.p.a.

3. **Forestry:**	Species distribution: Sitka Spruce: 43%
	        Japanese Larch: 20%
	        Scots Pine: 9%
	        Norway Spruce: 6%
	        European Larch: 5%
	        Other Conifers: 5%
	        Broadleaves: 12%

4. **Production:**	Conifer cycle now produces 10 000 tonnes of timber p.a. increased annually by 250 tonnes of thinnings. When in full production, the forest will yield three times this volume in perpetuity.

5. **Markets:**	Presently: Sawmill logs: 15%
	    Paper pulp: 40%
	    Posts and stakes: 35%
	    Asstd. products: 10%

6. **Farming:**	All fell land on the former farms has been planted, there are now 4 farms (264 ha. in total) whereas there were 7 (1225 ha) in 1937.
7. **Wildlife:**	1% is set aside for wildlife with habitat preservation to maintain a 'balance of wildlife' in the forest area.
8. **Multiple Use:**	Zoning policy is in practice to allow forestry development alongside farming, wildlife, recreation and tourism.

7.11 Grizedale Forest: basic facts

result of improvements in the motorway network, and ever-increasing car-ownership (Fig. 7.12). The great majority of these visitors regard the Lake District's scenery as being its main attraction, and in certain 'honeypot' areas, this has caused considerable management problems. One of the most popular of these 'honeypots' lies in the southern part of the Park at Tarn Hows, (Fig. 7.13) between Ambleside and Coniston, where the 13 hectare tarn, and magnificient panoramic views towards the central Lake District, combined to attract over half a million visitors each year in the early 1970s. This figure grew at a rate of 5% each year between 1972 and 1975. The pattern of increasing visitor use, accompanied by the erosion

1955:	3 million
1960:	5.5 million
1965:	9 million
1970:	12 million
1975:	14 million
1980:	20 million

7.12 Car ownership in the U.K. 1955–1980

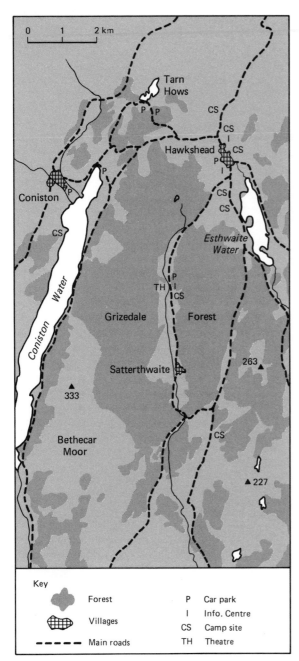

7.13 Grizedale Forest

of surface vegetation and gullying along the steeply sloping access paths from the existing car parks to the side of the tarn, gave rise to the need for a management plan to prevent further deterioration of the site (Fig. 7.14). The National Trust, the owners of the site, undertook a series of re-seeding experiments and consulted widely before deciding on a plan involving the closure of one of the car parks to improve visual amenity,

directing visitors instead along one of the prepared footpaths. This permitted the restoration of the vegetation cover in the heavily trampled and gullied areas, and the provision of information via notice boards, and small, unobstrusive, signs. In this way, they hope to maintain the levels of visitor use without further deterioration of the site.

Throughout all of the land-use controversies mentioned earlier the Lake District Special Planning Board has to bear in mind the needs of the local people in an area which has several of the symptoms of rural decline: falling employment in traditional industries, increasing 'second home' ownership, and the continued out-migration of young people, (Fig. 7.15). Amidst all of these problems, it also has to act as conservator of a truly majestic landscape.

11. Using an atlas:
    a) describe the situation of the Lake District within England;
    b) relate this situation to the locations of the major conurbations and the motorway network;
    c) compare the heights of the mountains in the area to the heights of the highest mountains in Scotland, Wales and elsewhere in England.

12. Why was the Lake District an obvious choice as one of the earliest National Parks?

13. List any land-use conflicts (Fig. 7.8) or conserve/develop inquiries which you have heard of recently and identify the main issues involved.

14. In 1936 the Forestry Commission and the Council for the Protection of Rural England agreed that an area of 777 km² of the central Lake District should never be forested. Bearing this in mind, and with the aid of Fig. 7.9, describe the distribution of Forestry Commission land in the Lake District.

15. Describe and explain the consequences of the increase in car ownership shown in Fig. 7.12 for areas such as the Lake District.

16. a) Name any other examples of 'honeypot' tourist sites you know of.
    b) Choose one of these which you know well or can find out about, and describe any signs of deterioration in the site, and attempts made to rectify this.

17. Study Fig. 7.15.
    a) Identify any pattern to the areas experiencing a decrease in young people between 1961-71.
    b) Suggest some methods which might be tried to attempt to reverse this loss of population.

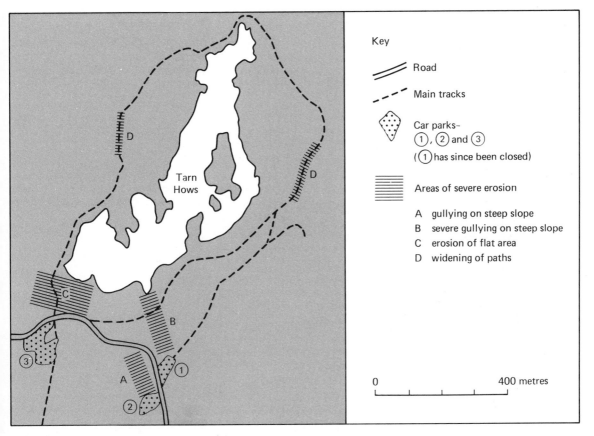

7.14 Tarn Hows

Key

Road

Main tracks

Car parks—
① , ② and ③
(① has since been closed)

Areas of severe erosion

A gullying on steep slope
B severe gullying on steep slope
C erosion of flat area
D widening of paths

0   400 metres

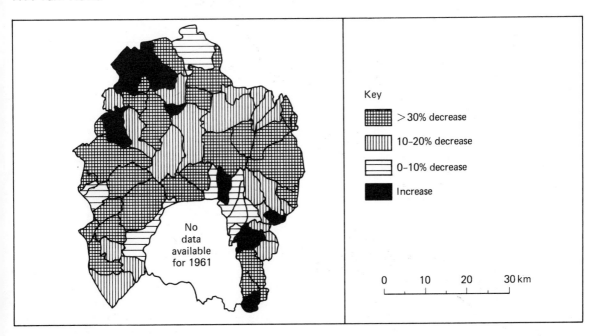

7.15 Lake District population change: comparison of 5–14 age group in 1961 with 15–24 age group in 1971

Key

>30% decrease

10–20% decrease

0–10% decrease

Increase

0   10   20   30 km

8

Planning for recreation in the countryside

Increased leisure time and mobility have added greatly to recreational pressures on the country-side this century. One of the first organisations to recognise this was the Forestry Commission which opened their first Forest Park (Figs. 7.3, 7.4) in Argyll in 1935. However, recreational pressures have been mounting, not just on the remoter, wilder areas of Britain, but also on areas of countryside near to our large towns and cities. In an attempt to cater for these recreational demands, Country Parks have been created. The legislation involved, the 'Countryside Acts' of 1967 and 1968, encouraged local authorities all over the British Isles to open Country Parks.

Most Country Parks lie fairly close to towns and cities and provide opportunities for both passive pursuits such as picnicking or taking a short walk in peaceful, rural surroundings, and more active pursuits such as pony trekking, sailing or orienteering. Country Parks vary enormously in size and character and most have a ranger service whose duties include the provision of advice, assistance and information to the public, patrolling, conservation and survey work. The three case studies which follow reflect this great diversity, especially in recreational pressure and landscape.

1. Suggest why recreational pressures on the countryside have increased in recent years.

2. Country Parks have been said to fulfill 'an interceptor role'. Explain what this might be.

3. Referring to Fig. 8.1 comment on the distribution of Country Parks in Britain in relation to the main centres of population.

John Muir Country Park

One of the largest Country Parks in Scotland, extending to some 675 hectares, is John Muir Country Park which occupies a coastal location in East Lothian, some 45 km to the east of Edinburgh. The Park is named after a native of

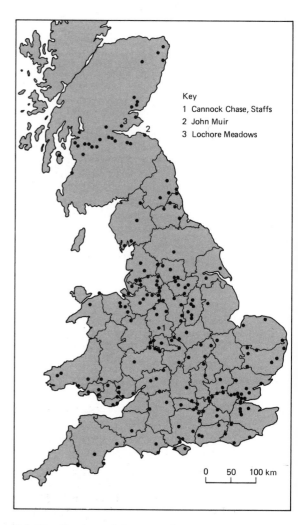

Key
1 Cannock Chase, Staffs
2 John Muir
3 Lochore Meadows

0   50   100 km

8.1 Distribution of Country Parks in Britain

Dunbar (the town, population 5700, which adjoins the eastern end of the Park), who emigrated at the age of 11 and later became one of the 'founding fathers' of the National Park movement in the U.S.A.

Prior to the designation of the John Muir

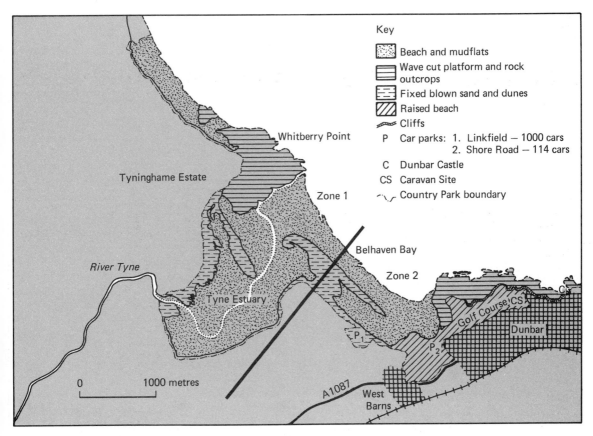

8.2 John Muir Country Park

Country Park by the Countryside Commission for Scotland in October 1976, the land which it now occupies was only partly owned by East Lothian District Council. In order to extend the area proposed for the Park, and the landscape variety it encompassed, several access and leasing agreements were signed with landowners, most notably the local Tyninghame Estate (Fig. 8.2) and the Crown Estate Commissioners. Four types of TOPOGRAPHY can be identified within the Country Park (Fig. 8.2):

1. The VOLCANIC STOCK at Whitberry Point, surrounded by an extensive WAVE-CUT PLATFORM, and with a long sandy beach bounded by dunes to the west.
2. The Tyne Estuary, with its associated SAND SPIT, SAND BAR and SALT MARSH.
3. The largely sandy expanse of Belhaven Bay with adjoining sand dunes and links (Fig. 8.3).
4. The massive old red sandstone and TUFF cliffs and WAVE-CUT PLATFORM along the shoreline at Dunbar (Fig. 8.4)

Such varied topography inevitably provides widely differing habitats for vegetation and wildlife, some of which are more ecologically sensitive than others. This had previously been recognised as far back as 1952 when an area including Belhaven Bay and part of the Tyninghame Estate had been declared a 'Site of Special Scientific Interest'. Similarly, certain management priorities had to be identified when the Country Park was created which resulted in the establishment of two broad zones where contrasting policies have been put into effect.

In the first of these, (Zone 1 on Fig. 8.2), in the western part of the Park, the emphasis has been placed upon conservation and public access has not been encouraged. Before the designation of the Country Park, a car park (P2 on Fig. 8.2), caravan site, and golf course were already in existence in what is now the eastern end of the Park (Zone2 on Fig. 8.2) and here various additional facilities, including another car park and toilets, children's adventure playground and an information board have been provided. By effectively zoning the Park in this way it has been

8.3 Belhaven Bay

possible to move some way toward the primary management objectives:

Zone 1: 'To conserve the present range of geological and geomorphological features, plant and animal communities'.

Zone 2: 'To provide the opportunity for public recreation in an area with a high landscape quality. The recreation will be dependent upon this quality and should not materially affect it by reducing its value'.

One of the major roles of the ranger service in John Muir Country Park has been to work towards the attainment of these management objectives. Their work now involves more than merely providing the public with basic information. It has sought to actively involve the public through the provision of interpretive pamphlets, and litter bags, taking guided walks, often with specialist themes, and conducting school and other parties around the Park as well as undertaking repair work where necessary. Recreational use of this area of the East Lothian coastline is nothing new. Long before the John Muir Country Park was created, specialist

pursuits such as horse riding, wildfowling and sand yachting took place and all of these had to be catered for when the original park management plan was drawn up. Dunbar Castle, with its historic associations, lies at the southern end of the Park (Fig. 8.2) and itself attracts many visitors each year. In an attempt to monitor recreational and visitor use of the Park, questionnaire surveys were carried out each year between 1977 and 1980 at various of the car parks. The cumulative results in reply to one question: "What were your reasons for coming here today?" are tabulated in Fig. 8.5. The relatively small numbers involved in the table, admittedly based on surveys undertaken on only a few days each year, do begin to suggest that this Country Park is one which is under relatively little recreational pressure at present. This fact has been further confirmed by a decision not to undertake further surveys as they simply have not proved necessary. Nevertheless, the situation may change later this decade as the area becomes more easily accessible from Edinburgh with the completion of new by-pass roads along the A1 trunk road reducing journey times to considerably less than an hour.

8.4 The coast at Dunbar

4. Explain the significance of the name 'John Muir' to the park movement world-wide, and its specific relevance to Dunbar in Scotland.

5. Why was a 'zoning policy' adopted in the management of John Muir Country Park (Fig. 8.2)?

6. Describe and classify as active or passive forms of recreation, the reasons given in Table 8.5 for visiting the John Muir Country Park.

7. Refer to the extract below (and Fig. 8.5) from the *East Lothian Courier* (20.1.84), the area's local newspaper. Suggest why widespread opposition has been expressed against this proposal and which particular local groups are likely to have objected:
"East Lothian M.P. John Home Robertson has called on local authorities, amenity bodies and conservationists to get together to save a section of the East Lothian coastline from 'disaster'.

The M.P., along with both East Lothian District Council and Lothian Regional Council is concerned that a scheme to win two million tonnes of marine sand and gravel off the John Muir Country Park in the Forth poses a threat to marine life and the general amenity of the area."

1. Picknicking	140
2. Walking	105
3. Walking dog	44
4. Swimming	44
5. Sunbathing	38
6. Bird-watching	30
7. Pleasure driving	29
8. Other nature studies	18
9. Photography	16
10. Fishing	6
11. Others	99

8.5 Reasons for visiting John Muir Country Park 1977–80, cumulative results

Cannock Chase Country Park

In contrast to John Muir Country Park in Scotland, which at present appears to be under relatively little recreational pressure, the area known as Cannock Chase in the English Midlands has been under increasing pressure for at least the last thirty years. Located on the northern fringe of the West Midlands conurbations (see Fig. 8.1), it forms by far the largest of the few areas of open space between Birmingham and the Pennines. As such it is a natural magnet for the 3.5 million people who can easily make a half-day trip to Cannock Chase along the M6 and its various tributary motorways.

The wild landscape which was a Royal Forest in medieval times has suffered considerable change over the centuries so that the semi-wild area of countryside which remains today is much smaller than it was then. The little that remains has been recognised as an 'Area of Outstanding Natural Beauty' and within it lies one of the country's largest Country Parks, extending to 1054 hectares (Fig. 8.6).

Physically, Cannock Chase is a northerly extension of the Midland Plateau which lies largely above 150 metres and is roughly triangular in shape. Its scenic quality is derived largely from its flat summits, the convex slopes along the Chase edge and deeply incised north-south valleys (Fig. 8.7). On this foundation, a mantle of heath, oak woodland and valley bog vegetation has evolved over the centuries and has been partly replaced during this century by the creation of large forestry plantations. The vegetation cover on Cannock Chase has been further altered during this century by the virtual ending of traditional management of heaths using burning, sheep grazing and cutting. Fires in these areas, often accidental, have led to a proliferation of bracken and the prevention of tree growth. Human influence is also very evident in the ugly scars left by a now much-depleted coal mining industry and by quarrying for sand and gravel. Even the remnants of military use of Cannock Chase earlier this century are still to be found in places and a firing range, to the east of the Park, is still in occasional use.

Rights of public access to Cannock Chase have existed since feudal times and these now extend over some 1374 hectares in eleven separate areas. Most of the trips made to Cannock Chase are for

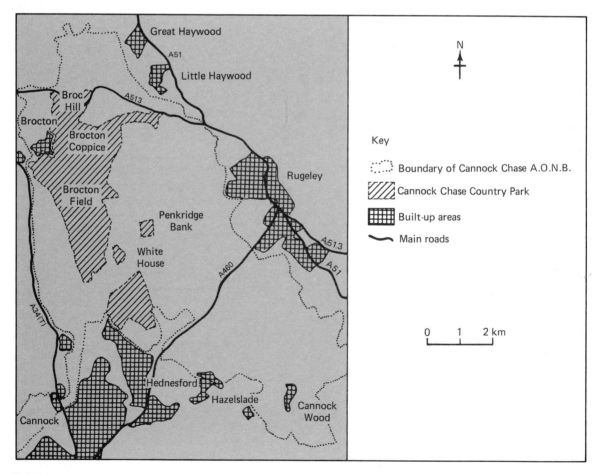

8.6 Cannock Chase

informal recreation, with 70% of visitors coming from within a 24 km radius of the Park. The great majority arrive by car, and at summer peaks over 10 000 visitors a day can be expected. This obviously placed the most popular areas of Cannock Chase Country Park, especially along its sloping edges and the river valley, under great pressure, and required some degree of management. As a result, the Countryside Commission funded an intensive research programme which resulted in a Management Plan for the Park, and also to act as a model plan for use by those in charge of the development of Country Parks elsewhere.

Research into the recreational use of Cannock Chase has revealed some interesting patterns. It appears that by far the largest number of visitors come by car (96%), in family groups of three to six, and with children. Most of the families (73% of weekend visitors) belong to the three highest socio-economic groups (professional, managerial and skilled manual or non-manual workers), and seem to come from elements of society who have continued their education at school for a relatively long time. The typical half-day trip to the Chase is often a fairly short duration, with 80% of the visitors staying for less than 3 hours.

Plotting the distribution of cars at peak times gives an impression of the intensity and distribution of visitor use (Fig. 8.7 a)) and from this map it can be seen that visitor distribution is far from even across the Park, and, given that the average visitor to the most popular areas remains within 400–800 metres of their car, the pressure on certain areas is intense. In particular, Milford Common (Fig. 8.7 b)) can be seen as an example of such pressure. It has been estimated that approximately half of the visitors to Cannock Chase call at Milford Common where a short walk up the neighbouring hills from the car park is

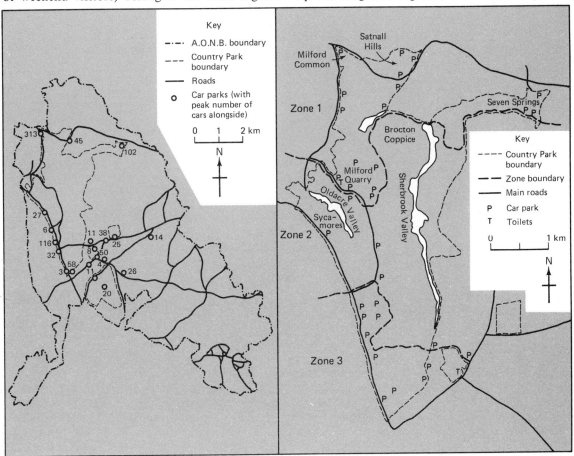

8.7 a) Cannock Chase Country Park showing car park use (peak numbers of cars on a 'normal' Summer Sunday afternoon)

8.7 b) Cannock Chase Country Park

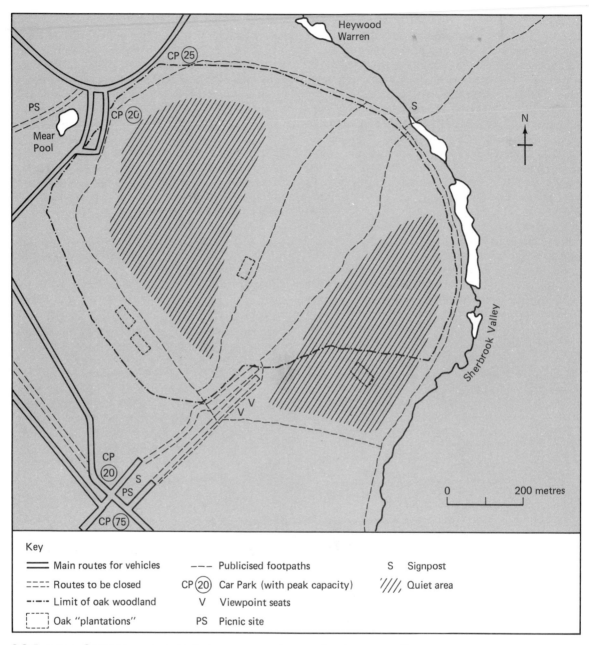

8.8 Brocton Coppice — proposals to ensure oak woodland regeneration

rewarded by spectacular views over surrounding landscape. The trampling effect of so many feet on the relatively steep slopes and paths with very thin soil cover, compounded by the erosive action of rainwater after storms, resulted in extensive gullying. These gullies expanded laterally as people walked along their fringes rather than on the loose, pebbly surface. In consequence a programme of rehabilitation has been necessary involving footpath restoration and the construction of steps, designed to blend in with the landscape. Progressive vegetation damage had also taken place in and around the car park, areas which are now periodically cordoned off to allow for regeneration of vegetation. Another way of diffusing the intensive visitor pressure in sites such as Milford Common is to provide information about other areas of the Park which have the capacity to absorb more visitors without environmental damage taking place. As Fig. 8.7 a) indicates, there are many parts of the Chase which remain virtually unvisited.

In certain of these areas the intrusion of vast numbers of visitors would be most unwelcome. Such an area is Brocton Coppice (Fig. 8.8), some 85 hectares of ancient oak woodland which lies fairly close to several major routes across the Chase. This is thought to be the last remnant of Cank Forest, and a plan has been devised by the local authority to transplant oak seedlings grown in a local nursery at various points around the woodland fringe in an attempt to ensure the survival of this unique oak woodland area. The seedlings are grown from acorns collected from the old woodlands, thus ensuring the genetic continuation of the oak population. In an attempt to reconcile the recreational pressures on Cannock Chase with the continuing need for conservation of flora and fauna, the management plan adopted by Staffordshire County Council proposed a 'zoning' policy similar to that in use at John Muir Country Park in Scotland. The Cannock Chase plan identifies three zones (Fig. 8.7 b)), which accepts that in certain areas recreational uses should take priority (Zone 1 on Fig. 8.7 b)), with nature conservation paramount in certain other areas (Zone 2), and with a third zone (Zone 3) designated for low density recreational use. Setting the boundaries between these zones was a major problem for the planners. One special provision was the attempt to decrease visitor pressure in Zone 2 by reducing significantly existing car parking places, whilst compensating for this reduction by creating new car parks in Zones 1 and 3. These measures should allow the managers of Cannock Chase Country Park to better plan for the future of this unique resource in an area of England which is so highly urbanised.

8. Locate Cannock Chase with the aid of Fig. 8.1 and an atlas and suggest why the Park is under such recreational pressure.

9. Why have the fringe areas of the Park been under such pressure?

10. What management problems result at peak visiting times and at the most popular locations?

11. Explain why the zoning policy adopted at Cannock Chase was rather different to that used at John Muir Country Park.

Lochore Meadows Country Park

The part of central Fife known as Lochore Meadows, (Fig. 8.1) was largely an agricultural landscape until the end of the nineteenth century when the first pits were sunk in the area. In the early twentieth century the landscape suffered the ravages of coal mining as six pits were opened up and the area became littered with their debris. By the mid 1960s (Fig. 8.9) all of the ugly features associated with old mining landscapes were to be found, all crammed into a very small area.

The collapse of the abandoned underground workings caused widespread subsidence and flooding of large areas of land such as Loch Ore as well as other smaller areas of water (Fig. 8.9). Closure of the last of the six collieries in the early 1960s left derelict pit-head buildings and silent winding gear, dangerous slurry ponds, and occasional rows of blackened miners' houses, all of which were surrounded by towering spoil heaps, some still on fire. At that point, the name Lochore 'Meadows' seemed tragically inappropriate and, although it only extended to 10 sq km, identified an area which had seriously blighted the landscape of central Fife. The county council, now Fife Regional Council, had previous experience of several small-scale reclamation schemes and resolved to undertake a massive, six-phase land renewal programme in the Lochore Meadows area. This aimed to improve the quality of the environment for local people, and make it more attractive to prospective employers in an unemployment black-spot area. Each phase of the scheme was undertaken independently, but was designed to contribute to an overall plan which sought to provide 'new' land for industry, agriculture and forestry and to create a Country Park.

As Fig. 8.11 indicates, perhaps the major problem faced throughout the scheme, was the moving, or regrading, of millions of cubic metres of colliery waste which had been piled up into unnatural shapes, to better blend in with the surrounding landscape.

At the heart of the area transformed lies the Lochore Meadows Country Park (Fig. 8.10) which now provides a range of recreational pursuits for local people and visitors alike. Traditionally fishing had been one of the most popular sports amongst the mining communities of the area and Loch Ore has been stocked with mature trout to cater for this demand. Sailors and canoeists also make use of the loch and a network of footpaths has been laid out around the Park. A golf course

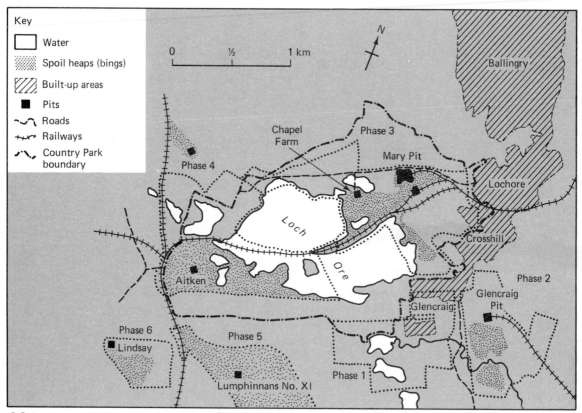

8.9 Lochore Meadows in the mid 1960s

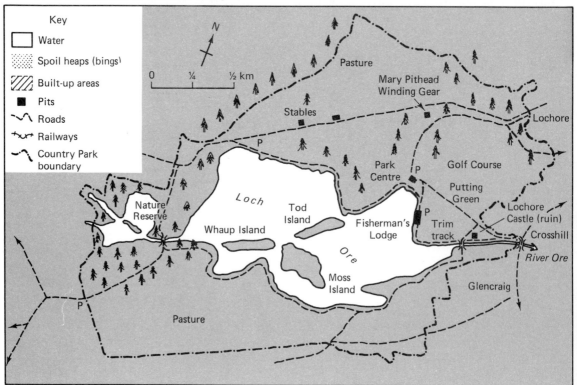

8.10 Lochore Meadows today

Phases and Dates	Area involved and Volume of Waste Regraded	Rehabilitation
Phase 1: 1967–68	72.8 ha. 191 000 m³	Flooded land drained and infilled with waste. New course cut for Loch Fitty Burn. Remains of South Glencraig village and Nellie Colliery buildings demolished. Grass sown. Industrial use today.
Phase 2: May 1969– Sept. 1970	83.4 ha. 1 529 000 m³	Spoil heaps from Nellie and Glencraig collieries regraded, used to fill slurry ponds. River Ore and Loch Fitty Burns cleared out. Top soil spread, grass sown. Area now leased to local farmers.
Phase 3: Nov. 1971– Oct. 1973	233 ha. 650 000 m³	Demolition of Mary Colliery, except for pithead winding gear, regrading of spoil heaps, waste used to build up banks of Loch Ore, lowered by earlier clearing of river. Top soil spread, grass sown, trees planted. Now centrepiece of Country Park.
Phase 4: Jan. 1973– May 1974	171 ha. 1 000 000 m³	Disused mineral railway across Loch Ore was cut to form several islands. Disused Aitken Colliery demolished and spoil heaps regraded. Infilling of slurry ponds Water-filled area of subsidence to west of Loch Ore left as nature reserve (now part of Country Park) Top soil spread, grass sown. Mostly agricultural use today
Phase 5: Sept. 1974– Aug. 1975	39 ha. 900 000 m³	Lumphinnans No. XI Colliery waste heaps regraded. Pit shafts and surface mine located and concrete capped. Followed by agricultural operations.
Phase 6:	40 ha. 565 000 m³	Final phase involved regrading of Lindsay Colliery spoil heaps where temperatures exceeded 1000°C. at times, and the concrete capping of shafts and surface mines. Area now used for agriculture.

8.11 Phases of the Lochore Meadows Scheme

has been provided in the north east of the area and a ranger service and the steady improvement of facilities have contributed to its appeal. The Country Park now attracts more than 1000 visitors a day in mid-summer, with a total in excess of 100 000 in 1983.

This bold and imaginative land reclamation scheme is by no means the only one of its kind in Britain, one on a similar scale has recently been completed in the Rother Valley on the border between Derbyshire and South Yorkshire. These schemes illustrate how areas of landscape so seriously despoiled in the past can be rehabilitated to once more provide important assets for local communities and the national interest alike.

12. Why was the name Lochore 'Meadows' so inappropriate to that part of central Fife in the mid 1960s?

13. Compare Figs. 8.9 and 8.10. Describe the transformation in the area as a result of the Lochore Meadows Scheme.

14. From Fig. 8.11 suggest what caused the major problems throughout the scheme's six phases.

15. From the three Country Park case studies in this chapter:
   a) Make a list of the features which are common to all of them;
   b) Attempt to draw your own 'model' of a Country Park using your list compiled in (a).

Glossary

ADVANCING COASTLINE	a coastline where the land is building out into the sea
ALLUVIUM	material carried down by a river
ANTICLINE	the arch or crest of a fold in rock strata
AREA OF OUTSTANDING NATURAL BEAUTY	an area designated by the Countryside Commission because of its beautiful scenery
ARETE	a sharp serrated ridge between two adjacent corries
AUREOLE	rock surrounding a mass of Instrusive Rock which has been changed by great heat and/or pressure
BATHOLITH	a dome shaped mass of igneous rock formed originally below the earth's surface
BLOW HOLE	a hole in the roof of a coastal cave through which air and seawater are forced with some ferocity
BOSS	a relatively small batholith of a circular shape
CARBONIFEROUS	the geological era when coal was extensively formed
CHEMICAL WEATHERING	the decay and disintegration of the rocks of the earth's crust by exposure to the atmosphere and the elements
CLINT	a ridge of bare rock betwen fissures or grykes on a limestone "pavement"
CLITTER	frost shattered rock fragments which have broken off from tors in granite areas
COMMON LAND	a piece of land belonging to the local community as a whole which is open to common use
CORRASION	the mechanical wearing away of a river's bed and banks by the solid material carried by a river
CORRIE	a deep steepsided basin-shaped hollow found in high mountain areas formed through erosion by snow and ice
CORROSION	the wearing away of rocks by chemical action e.g. by solution
CUESTA	see escarpment
CWM	see corrie
DENUDATION	the wearing away of the land by various natural agencies e.g. sun, wind, rain, frost, ice
DEPOSITION	the laying down of solid material which has been carried by some natural agency e.g. river, wind and glacier
DESIGNATION	the identification of areas for conservation purposes
DOWNS	open, hilly land, mainly treeless, sparsely covered with soil and mainly used for sheep grazing in the past. Normally associated with chalk landscapes
DRY VALLEY	a valley in which the stream has disappeared completely or flows on the surface only occasionally
EMERGENT COASTLINE	an area of coast where the land is rising in relation to the sea
ENCLOSURE	subdividing large areas of land by walls or hedges
ESCARPMENT	a ridge with an identifiable steep (or scarp) side and gentle (or dip) side

ESTUARY	the mouth of a river where it widens out and where fresh and sea-water mix
EXTRUSIVE ROCKS	rocks formed by magma solidifying on the earth's surface e.g. volcanic lava
FLUVIOGLACIAL	the action of melt water streams below the snout of a glacier or edge of an ice sheet
GEO	a gully or creek
GLACIAL TROUGH	a long deep glaciated valley
GRYKE	a fissure between clints or ridges on the surface of the rock on a limestone ''pavement''
HANGING VALLEY	a tributary valley which enters a main valley from a considerable height, particularly common in glaciated areas
HERITAGE COASTS	areas of coastline designated by the Countryside Commission because of their outstanding nature
HIGHLAND GLACIATION	the action of glaciers in mountain area
ISOSTATIC UPLIFT	part of theory that different areas of the earth's crust are in equilibrium - one part rising, or uplifting, as another falls
IGNEOUS	rocks which have solidified from molten magma
IMPERMEABLE	rocks which do not allow water to soak into them either through pores(non-porous) or cracks (impervious)
INBYE	improved, cultivated land near to the farm buildings
INFRASTRUCTURE	the network of basic services e.g. roads, water supply which sustain an industrial area or urban centre
INTRUSIVE ROCKS	igneous rocks which solidified from magma before reaching the earth's surface
JURASSIC LIMESTONE	a type of limestone formed during the geological period of the same name which forms escarpments e.g. the Cotswolds in England
KARST	a carboniferous limestone landscape with characteristic underground drainage, caverns etc
LANDAM	a primitive type of farming similar to shifting cultivation
LIMESTONE	a rock consisting essentially of calcium carbonate. There are several different forms e.g. jurassic, oolitic and carboniferous
LIMESTONE PAVEMENT	a horizontal area of exposed carboniferous limestone above a cliff face or scar
LIMESTONE SCAR	a steep, bare rock face; a crag found on carboniferous limestone rock
LONG DISTANCE FOOTPATHS	cross-country walking routes planned by the Countryside Commission
MEANDER	a curve or bend in a river
METAMORPHIC ROCKS	rocks which were originally igneous or sedimentary but which have been changed due to the action of heat, pressure or water
MISFIT STREAM	a river that appears to be too small to have carved out the valley through which it flows
MOUNTAIN LIMESTONE	rocks of the limestone type found in high areas
NATIONAL PARK	an extensive area of largely open countryside which is subject to strict planning controls
NATIONAL PARK DIRECTION AREA	land in Scotland designated as being suitable for the creation of a National Park
NATIONAL SCENIC AREA	land in Scotland of great beauty which is subject to certain planning controls
OPEN CAST	a form of mining which involves the removal of surface layers prior to the extraction of the mineral
PERIGLACIAL	climatic conditions experienced around the fringes of an ice-sheet
PERMEABLE	rocks which allow water to pass through

PERVIOUS	rocks which allow water to pass through by means of cracks or joints
POROUS	rocks which allow water to pass through by means of pores
PYRAMIDAL (OR HORNED) PEAK	a sharp mountain top formed as a result of corrie formation near the summit
RETREATING COASTLINE	an area of coastline which is being gradually eroded away
RIA	a drowned river valley
RIBBON LAKE	a long narrow glacial lake found in the bottom of a glaciated valley
SALT MARSH	a boggy area, which is sometimes flooded by the sea
SAND BAR	a ridge of sand or shingle which has built out from a coastline often across the mouth of a river
SAND SPIT	a narrow low-lying area of sand or shingle which projects out from a coastline
SCREE	small sharp and angular rock fragments which are formed due to frost shattering on cliff faces
SECOND HOME	a holiday house which is not a permanent residence and is only occupied part of the year
SEDIMENTARY	rocks formed originally under water as a result of materials built up in layers on the sea floor
SINK	a surface depression often found in limestone regions
SOLIFLUCTION	freeze/thaw processes which often result in downslope movement of surface materials
SOLUTION HOLLOWS	the beginnings of sea-caves along a cliff coastline
STALACTITE	a column which extends downwards from the roof of a limestone cavern
STALAGMITE	a column which extends upwards from the floor of a limestone cavern
SUBMERGENCE	falling in the level of an area of the land in relation to the sea until it falls below sea level
SWALLOW HOLE	the vertical shaft which forms the entrance to an underground cave system in a limestone region
TARN	a small lake or loch which occupies the floor of a corrie
TOPOGRAPHY	shape of the land
TUFF	an igneous rock formed from consolidated volcanic ash or dust
U-SHAPED VALLEY	a valley with a flat floor and steep sides formed by a glacier
VOLCANIC STOCK	a small protruding area of volcanic rock
WATER TABLE	the level of water within any area of rock
WAVE CUT PLATFORM	a shelf of rock on a coastline which has been worn down by wave action
WEATHERING	the breaking down of the rocks on the earth's surface
WILDERNESS	see 'wildscape'
WILDSCAPE	areas of unimproved land, mostly moorland and heath, found largely in the higher parts of the U.K.